Wiley Keys to Success

How to Build a
Super Vocabulary

Beverly Ann Chin is Professor of English, Director of the English Teaching Program, former Director of the Montana Writing Project, and a former President of the National Council of Teachers of English.

Dr. Chin is a nationally recognized leader in English language arts standards, curriculum instruction, and assessment. Many schools and states call upon her to help them develop programs in reading and writing across the curriculum. Dr. Chin has edited and written numerous books and articles in the field of English language arts. She is the author of *On Your Own: Writing* and *On Your Own: Grammar.*

Wiley Keys to Success

How to Build a Super Vocabulary

Beverly Ann Chin, Ph.D.
Series Consultant

WILEY

John Wiley & Sons, Inc.

Published by John Wiley & Sons, Inc., Hoboken, New Jersey
Published simultaneously in Canada

For general information about our other products and services, please contact our Customer Care Department within the United States at (800) 762-2974, outside the United States at (317) 572-3993 or fax (317) 572-4002.

Wiley also publishes its books in a variety of electronic formats. Some content that appears in print may not be available in electronic books. For more information about Wiley products, visit our web site at www.wiley.com.

Library of Congress Cataloging-in-Publication Data:

How to build a super vocabulary / Beverly Ann Chin, series consultant.
  p. cm.
 Includes index.
 ISBN 0-471-43157-5 (pbk. : alk. paper)
 1. Vocabulary.
 PE1449.H588 2004
 428.1—dc22   2004002248

Printed in the United States of America

10 9 8 7 6 5 4 3 2 1

DEAR STUDENTS

Welcome to the **WILEY KEYS TO SUCCESS** series! The books in this series are practical guides designed to help you be a better student. Each book focuses on an important area of schoolwork, including building your vocabulary, studying and doing homework, writing research papers, taking tests, and more.

Each book contains seven chapters—the keys to helping you improve your skills as a student. As you understand and use each key, you'll find that you will enjoy learning more than ever before. As a result, you'll feel more confident in your classes and be better prepared to demonstrate your knowledge.

I invite you to use the **WILEY KEYS TO SUCCESS** series at school and at home. As you apply each key, you will open the doors to success in school as well as to many other areas of your life. Good luck, and enjoy the journey!

Beverly Ann Chin, Series Consultant
Professor of English
University of Montana, Missoula

Note to Teachers, Librarians, and Parents

The **WILEY KEYS TO SUCCESS** series is a series of handbooks designed to help students improve their academic performance. Happily, the keys can open doors for everyone—at home, in school, at work.

Each book is an invaluable resource that offers seven simple, practical steps to mastering an important aspect of schoolwork, such as building vocabulary, studying and doing homework, taking tests, and writing research papers. We hand readers seven keys—or chapters—that show them how to increase their success as learners—a plan intended to build lifelong learning skills. Reader-friendly graphics, self-assessment questions, and comprehensive appendices provide additional information.

Helpful features scattered throughout the books include "Getting It Right," which expands on the text with charts, graphs, and models; "Inside Secret," which reveals all-important hints, rules, definitions, and even warnings; and "Ready, Set, Review," which makes it easy for students to remember key points.

WILEY KEYS TO SUCCESS *are designed to ensure that all students have the opportunity to experience success*. Once students know achievement, they are more likely to become independent learners, effective communicators, and critical thinkers. Many readers will want to use each guidebook by beginning with the first key and progressing systematically to the last key. Some readers will select the keys they need most and integrate what they learn with their own routines.

As educators and parents, you can encourage students to use the books in this series to assess their own strengths and weaknesses as learners. Using students' responses and your own observations of their study skills and habits, you can help students develop positive attitudes, set realistic goals, form successful schedules, organize materials, and monitor their own academic progress. In addition, you can discuss how adults use similar study strategies and communication skills in their personal and professional lives.

We hope you and your students will enjoy the **WILEY KEYS TO SUCCESS** series. We think readers will turn to these resources time and time again. By showing students how to achieve everyday success, we help children grow into responsible, independent young adults who value their education—and into adults who value learning throughout their lives.

Beverly Ann Chin, Series Consultant
Professor of English
University of Montana, Missoula

CONTENTS

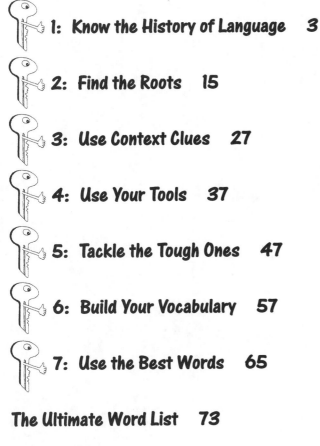

INTRODUCTION

The English language is huge, immense, enormous, titanic, prodigious. (All of these words mean "very large.") The big, fat unabridged dictionaries have about half a million entry words. Language experts estimate that English may have as many as a million words if you count scientific and technical terms. And like all living languages, English keeps growing all the time.

So how many English words do you know already? Probably many thousands. But just as you wouldn't stay with the vocabulary you had when you were two or three years old, you won't stay with the one you have now. Your vocabulary will keep growing as you meet new words in your reading and hear them in conversations, on radio, or on TV.

Your vocabulary is directly related to your success in school. That's why there are so many vocabulary questions on state and national standardized tests. Readers who evaluate your writing on essay tests also focus on your vocabulary, to make sure you use words precisely and correctly.

The book you are holding, *How to Build a Super Vocabulary*, is a resource and reference book that can help you enlarge your vocabulary. It introduces you to many new words to use when you write, read, speak, and listen.

You can also learn strategies—systematic approaches—for discovering the meaning of unfamiliar words:

- Recognize different kinds of context clues that enable you to make an educated guess about the meaning of an unfamiliar word in your reading.

- Learn how a dictionary and a thesaurus can help expand your vocabulary, especially when you're writing.

- Recognize the meanings of some of the most familiar roots, prefixes, and suffixes. Those word parts will help you puzzle out the meaning of many unfamiliar English words.

- Put the new words you acquire to good use in your speaking and writing.

- Avoid some of the mistakes and mix-ups that can happen when you use English words.

At the back of this book, you'll find "The Ultimate Word List," a mini-dictionary of words that will help you focus on strengthening your personal weak spots. Some of these are words you're expected to know now. Others are words that you're challenged to learn. One long list has words from different content areas, and another contains words commonly found on standardized tests.

"The Ultimate Word List" is just a starting point. Use those words in sentences. Make them your own.

By the time you finish reading this book, your vocabulary will have grown considerably. You'll also have gained skills and strategies that you can apply to any unfamiliar word you meet—for the rest of your life.

KNOW THE HISTORY OF LANGUAGE

✓ **Theories About How Language Began**

✓ **How Language Changes**

✓ **Looking at Some Interesting Words**

Isn't it amazing that all over the world newborn babies grow up to speak the language that their parents speak? If you had been born in France, you'd be speaking French.

Maybe you can speak, read, write, or understand two languages. That would make you bilingual. (You'd be trilingual if you could speak three languages; some people speak even more.) Your native language, or "mother tongue," is the first language you learned, most likely the one you speak at home. Now you may be taking a foreign-language course in school.

Theories About How Language Began

Words give you power. They give you the ability to share your thoughts and ideas. Written words can help you tune in to the thoughts of people who lived long ago or who live far away. Words also help you to imagine anything—experiences you've never had and events far into the future. (For a sampling of some English words and the ideas they let you express, see the words on "The Ultimate Word List" at the back of this book.)

No one knows when or how language first began. *Linguists*, the experts who study language, have some theories, or ideas, about the origin of language.

Language as Instinct

Many modern linguists think the human brain is hard-wired for language. Your ability to speak and understand words is *instinctual*, meaning it comes naturally. This ability makes you different from all other species. Babies learn to speak spontaneously—without formal instruction. The babbling or nonsense sounds that infants make are part of learning the vocabulary and grammar of their native language.

Say It with Gestures

Some linguists believe that before people used language, they communicated with *gestures*, movements of their hands and arms. The earliest people conveyed meaning by making faces, pointing, motioning, or touching objects. Gradually, they began to use sounds that they agreed would stand for the objects around them. Those sounds were the first words.

Words enabled people to talk about things they could not see or touch. In the middle of summer, for instance, they could talk about the snow and ice that would come in winter. And even though the sun was shining brightly, they could talk about the moon and stars they could not see until nighttime.

The Bowwow Theory

This theory and the next two were popular during the nineteenth century but aren't endorsed by most linguists today. (Their names make fun of these theories.) Some people believed that language began when people imitated the sounds made by the things they were describing. *Roar*, *buzz*, and *crash*, for instance, are *echoic*, or *onomatopoeic*, words. That means the spoken words sound like the sounds they are describing.

According to the linguist Mario Pei, the sound of a sneeze is written differently in different languages. You'd write *ker-choo* in English, *gu-gu* in Japanese, *hah-chee* in Chinese, and *ap-chi* in Russian.

Yo-Ho, Heave-Ho Theory

Other linguists believed that language came from the sounds (grunting, groaning, and rhythmic chanting) that people made as they worked together at some task. No one knows what those grunts, groans, and chants sounded like. ("Yo ho, heave-ho" is a chant that sailors sometimes used as they pulled together on a rope.) For the earliest speakers, language was especially useful while hunting, sharing food, and protecting themselves from attacks.

The Pooh-Pooh Theory

The English naturalist Charles Darwin (1809–1882) believed that language developed from instinctive cries that humans made to express emotions, such as fear, anger, pleasure, and pain. For instance, you might say *"mmmm"* when you are licking a chocolate ice-cream cone or *"ow!"* when someone steps on your toe.

So What Do You Think?

Remember, those are all *theories*—guesses about why something happens. No one knows for sure why and how language began. Which theory about the origin of language makes the most sense to you? Why? Can you think of another explanation for the first human speech?

How Language Changes

Languages are changing and growing all the time. That's true not just for English but for every *living language*. (A living language is one that's still being spoken.) Languages change in three basic ways.

New Words Come

New words are coined—made up—to describe scientific discoveries and new inventions and experiences. Fax (short for *facsimile*) entered English in the 1980s, when the device for transmitting documents through phone lines was invented. Think of *e-mail, smog, software, robotics, laser,* and *hologram*—all those words came along in the late twentieth century.

Old Words Go

Gradually, words disappear because they are no longer used. *Thee, thou,* and *ye* are *archaic* (no-longer-used) forms of *you.* You might find the archaic ere (*before*) or o'er (*over*) in poetry but not in speech.

Meanings Change

A word may stay, but its meaning may change. Whoever could imagine that the word *bead* meant "prayer" when it began in Middle English? Or that there'd be this new meaning for the word *burn:* You can *burn* a CD from online music files. *Slang,* a form of informal speech, gives us a never-ending supply of new meanings for old words. *Cool,* for example, once referred only to temperature. For many decades, *cool* has meant "excellent" or "very good."

Looking at Some Interesting Words

Every word has a story. Most English words have come a long way through many languages. A dictionary tells a word's history in an *etymology* that's usually printed after the pronunciation and before the definitions. Etymologies trace the origin and development of words. They show a word's original language and form and other languages and forms the word has moved through as it has developed.

GETTING IT RIGHT

Nouns Become Verbs

One of the ways in which language changes is that words take on new meanings. Sometimes the part of speech also changes. For example, someone starts using a noun as a verb, and eventually that usage becomes widespread. Some words that started out as nouns and became verbs include babysit (from *babysitter*) and intuit (from *intuition*).

Here are some recent examples of verbs made from nouns.

- Will you please e-mail me the date and time of your arrival?
- Stacy's grandmother faxed her the recipe for potato pancakes.
- When he was searching for a job, Runar networked with his former classmates and everyone else he knew.
- Lauren hopes to broker a new contract with her employer.

Etymologies go backward in time. They begin with the most recent form of the word and go back to the oldest known form. Etymologies use abbreviations and symbols to tell a story about the word.

Fr = French	ME = Middle English	lit. = literally
Gr = Greek	OE = Old English	prob. = probably
L = Latin	< = derived from	? = unknown

Here's what the etymology of the English word *person* might look like:

person (PER·sun) *n.* [ME *persone* < OFr < L *persona*, lit., mask (esp. one worn by an actor), character, role, person, prob. < Etruscan *phersu*, mask]

Can you "translate" this etymology? Here's what it says: The English word *person* comes from the Middle English word *persone*, which in turn comes from an Old French word and before that from the Latin word *persona*. Literally, *persona* means "mask," especially one worn by an actor, so *persona* came to refer to a character, role, or person. Probably the word *persona* came from the Etruscan word *phersu*, which means "mask."

Wow! That's a lot of information packed into a two-line etymology. No wonder dictionary writers use abbreviations and symbols. You can read dictionary etymologies whenever you want to find out about a word's history. You can find a key to the abbreviations and symbols at the front of every dictionary.

Eponyms

How would you like to have a word named after you—not just any word, but a word you personally inspired? It's fun to learn about *eponyms*, words that have been named after real or mythical people. *Pennsylvania*, for example, is an eponym, named for the state's founder, William Penn. Here are some common eponyms:

- **boycott** *v.* to join with others in refusing to buy, use, or sell a product.

The story behind the word. Captain C. C. Boycott was a land agent in Ireland. In 1880, he raised the land rents so high that his tenants and neighbors joined together and refused to deal with him. It was the first boycott.

- **Ferris wheel** *n.* an amusement-park ride consisting of a gigantic vertical wheel that revolves on a fixed axle. Passengers ride in seats that hang between two parallel rims.

The story behind the word. George W. G. Ferris, an American engineer from Galesburg, Illinois, designed and built the first Ferris wheel ride for the World's Fair held in Chicago in 1893.

- **gerrymander** *v.* to redraw an election district to give one political party an advantage. The purpose of redrawing a voting district is to weaken the political power of ethnic, racial, or urban voters.

The story behind the word. Elbridge Gerry (1744–1814) signed the Declaration of Independence. Then, he served as governor of Massachusetts and U.S. vice president (1813–1814) under President James Madison. In 1812, while Gerry was still governor of Massachusetts, Essex County was redrawn to give his own political party an advantage. The redrawn district looked something like a salamander, so a political cartoonist coined the word *gerrymander* (*Gerry* + *mander*).

- **maverick** *n.* someone who acts independently. A maverick acts according to his or her beliefs, refusing to go along with what others are doing.

The story behind the word. Samuel Maverick (1803–1870), a Texas rancher, refused to brand his cattle despite the fact that all the other ranchers were branding theirs.

- **sandwich** *n.* two slices of bread with meat, cheese, fish, or other filling between them.

The story behind the word. John Montagu (1718–1792), the fourth earl of Sandwich, didn't want to stop playing cards at a gambling table. He ordered a servant to bring him roast beef wrapped in bread, and the sandwich was born.

- **sideburns** *n.* whiskers on a man's face in front of the ears, especially when no beard is worn.

INSIDE SECRET

Borrowed Words

When borrowed words become part of the English language, they often get a new pronunciation. For example, the word *denim*, the sturdy cotton material used for blue jeans, came from the French. It was originally *serge* (a type of cloth) *de Nîmes*, from Nîmes, the city where it was made. The French say "duh• NEEM," but Americans changed it to "DEN•im."

The story behind the word. During the Civil War, Union General Ambrose Everett Burnside (1824–1881) wore a mustache and side whiskers but shaved his chin clean. This style of beard was called *burnsides*, after the general. Eventually, the word order reversed to become *sideburns*.

Borrowed Words

Without borrowing, you wouldn't be eating cookies or coleslaw—they'd be called something else. English is a much richer language because of the many foreign words that it has borrowed. After the Norman Conquest of England in 1066, when French became the official language of the English government and the court, thousands of French words came into the English language.

Wherever people traveled, they found new animals, foods, places, and ideas that had been named in other languages. And they knew a good word when they heard or saw it. So English grew and grew, enriched by borrowed words from many different languages.

Here are some of the languages that have given us words and just a few of the many English words we've borrowed from them:

Borrowed Words

African   banana, bongo, chimpanzee, mumbo jumbo, yam
American Indian   chipmunk, moccasin, moose, powwow, raccoon
Arabic   algebra, assassin, coffee, cotton, jar, sofa
Chinese   china, silk, tea, typhoon
Dutch   boss, landscape, pickle, sketch, sled, split, stove, wagon
French   barber, detail, essay, government, justice, liberty, proof, ticket, treaty
German   delicatessen, dollar, hamburger, kindergarten, noodle, pretzel
Inuit (Eskimo)   anorak, igloo, kayak
Italian   balcony, carnival, piano, sonnet, spaghetti, umbrella
Old Norse   both, cake, freckles, happen, happy, leg, sky, take, ugly, want
Russian   cosmonaut, mammoth, parka, steppe
Scandinavian   geyser, gremlin, rug, ski
Spanish   alligator, barbecue, lasso, ranch, stampede, tomato

Ready, Set, *REVIEW*

Language History

1. Match each of the numbered words with the language that English borrowed it from. (At the end, every English word should be matched with one foreign language.) While you're at it, write a definition of each word. Then, use a dictionary to check your guesses.

1. bonanza	a. Spanish
2. banjo	b. Dutch
3. skunk	c. French
4. sleigh	d. Arabic
5. pretzel	e. American Indian
6. vogue	f. Italian
7. spaghetti	g. African
8. zero	h. Norwegian
9. ski	i. Hindi
10. shampoo	j. German

2. Do a little detective work. In a dictionary that shows etymologies, look up three of the words from the list below. First, discover what the word means. Then, use the etymology to decipher the story behind the word. You may need to look up a person's name, too. Tell each word's story to a friend or family member.

teddy bear	Bunsen burner	Geiger counter
Celsius	Fahrenheit	pasteurize

3. What language does each of the following English word come from? Use a dictionary to find each word's etymology.

zero   cookie   walrus   canyon   pasta
skunk   waffle   cockroach   potato   attorney

4. What's the story behind the name of your state? Many state names and other place-names come from American Indian languages. Check the etymology of your state's name in a dictionary to find out about it.

KEY 2

FIND THE ROOTS

✓ **Base Words and Roots**

✓ **Combining Forms**

✓ **Prefixes and Suffixes**

Some English words are short and snappy. But many English words are built from words and word parts that have been combined to make new words.

Recognizing word parts and knowing their meanings can help you unlock the meaning of many unfamiliar words. This chapter introduces you to three different kinds of basic word parts that carry a word's core meaning: *base words*, *roots*, and *combining forms*. You'll also meet two kinds of add-ons: *prefixes*, which come at the beginning, and *suffixes*, which come at the end, of a word.

Base Words and Roots

Learning new words is a lot easier when you find familiar parts in them. Learn to look for the most important part of a word, its base word or root. A *base word* is an ordinary English word to which prefixes and/or suffixes have been added. In the word *disappearance*, for example, the base word is *appear:*

dis- + **appear** + -ance = disappearance

Can you find the base word in *unforgettable* and in *research?*

Many English words are related: They come from the same root. A root is not a separate English word the way that a base word is.

Base Words and Roots

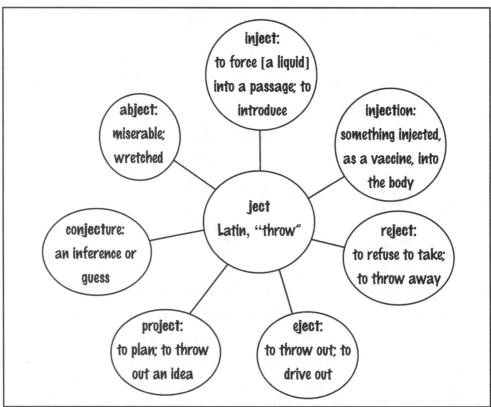

Instead, a *root* is a group of letters that carries a meaning from a different language, usually Greek or Latin.

BASE WORD   un**usual**
Usual is a base word.

WORD ROOT   re**cur**rent
Cur is a Latin root that means "run."

The word web on page 16 shows you a word *family*. All of the words are related because they come originally from the Latin root-*ject*, meaning "throw." You can see that some words have stayed close to the original meaning of the root while others have taken on new meanings.

INSIDE SECRET

The History of Words

When learning vocabulary words, you don't absolutely need to know which roots are Greek and which are Latin. But if you are someone who likes learning a little bit of history, you may find that kind of information interesting and even helpful. The more familiar you become with the stories behind words, the more easily you can remember the details about roots—and use them to make connections to other words.

GETTING IT RIGHT

Know Your Greek and Latin

This chart shows some common Greek and Latin roots, their meaning, and English words containing those roots.

Root	Meaning	Examples
-aqua-	water	aquarium, aquatic
-cede-, -ceed-	go, yield	precede, proceed
-cosm-	universe	cosmic, cosmonaut
-cred-, -credit-	believe	credible, credo
-curr-, -curs-	run	current, excursion
-dic-, dict-	say	diction, dictator
-duc-, -duct-	lead	conduct, educate
-fac-, -fic-	make, do	factory, fiction
-fer-	bring, carry	transfer, refer
-ject-	throw	reject, inject
-jud-, -jur-, -just-	law	judicial, jury, justice
-loc-	place	location, locate
-log-	word	dialogue, monologue
-lum-	light	luminous, illuminate
-luna-	moon	lunar, lunatic
-mater-, -matr-	mother	maternal, matriarch
-mort-	death	mortal, immortal
-pater-	father	paternity, paternal
-ped-	foot	pedal, pedestrian
-pend-	hang, weight	depend, pendulum
-pon-, -pos-	put, place	postpone, position
-port-	carry	transport, import
-rupt-	break	interrupt, erupt
-scribe-, -scrip-	write	describe, scripture
-sens-	feeling	sensation, sensitive
-spec-	see, look	spectator, spectacles
-tact-	touch	contact, tactile
-temp-	time	temporary, tempo
-therm-	heat	thermos, thermometer
-trans-	across	transport, transfer
-vid-	see	evidence, video
-viv-	life	vivid, revive

Combining Forms

Every time you pick up a *telephone* or ride in an *automobile* or look at a *photograph,* you use a combining form. Such words are called *combining forms* because they combine with other word forms or with prefixes or suffixes, or both, to form new words. Most combining forms come originally from ancient Latin and Greek words.

Combining Form	Meaning	Examples
anthropo-	man	anthropology
-archy	government, rule	monarchy, matriarchy
audio-	hearing, sound	audiocassette, audiovisual
auto-	self	automobile, autograph
biblio-	book	bibliography
chron-	time	chronology, chronic
geo-	earth	geography, geology
-gram	something written	telegram, grammar
-graph	something that writes or is written	phonograph, paragraph
hydro-	water	hydrogen, hydroelectric
-logy, -ology	science of, study of	ecology, psychology
mega-	very large, great	megabyte, megadose
-meter	instrument for measuring	speedometer, thermometer
micro-	small	microscope, microbe
mid-	middle	midway, midnight
mini-	very small	minivan, minibike
multi-	many	multicolored, multiethnic
omni-	all, everywhere	omnipresent, omniscient
-phobia	fear	claustrophobia
-phone	device producing sound	telephone, microphone
photo-	light	photograph, photosensitive
poly-	much, many	polygraph, polyunsaturated
psych-, psycho-	mind	psychology, psychic
-scope	instrument for seeing	microscope, telescope
tele-	at, over, or from a distance	telegraph, telephone

Prefixes and Suffixes

Just a few letters can make a world of difference. *Un-* added
to *happy* changes your mood to its opposite. *Mis-* added to *adventure*
turns an adventure into a disaster.

Think of prefixes and suffixes as attachments. They attach to the
beginning (prefix) or the end (suffix) of a base word or root to create a
new word. The general name that covers both prefixes and suffixes is
affix. An affix is a word part that is added to a base word to change its
meaning.

Prefixes Come at the Beginning

A *prefix* is a group of letters (one or two syllables) that attach to the beginning of a base word or root to create a new word. Prefixes have meanings that change the base word in a specific way:

re- (again) + play = replay (to play again)

semi- (half) + circle = semicircle (half a circle)

bi- (two) + weekly = biweekly (once every two weeks)

un- (not) + pleasant = unpleasant (not pleasant)

Here are some common prefixes with their meanings and some example words.

Prefix	Meaning	Examples
a-, ab-	not, without	atypical, amoral, abnormal
ante-	before	anteroom, antecedent
anti-	against, opposite	antiwar, antibody
arch-	main, chief	archenemy, archangel
bi-	two	bicycle, biweekly
circum-	around	circumference, circumstance
co-, com-, con-	with, together	coauthor, commit, conference
contra-	against	contrary, contradict
de-, dis-	opposite, down, away from	defrost, dishonest
ex-	out of, away from, former	extract, ex-president
fore-	before	foreground, foreknowledge
il-, im-, in-, ir-	not	illegal, impossible, inadequate, irresponsible
in-	into	invade, intrude
inter-	between, among	interstate, international
intra-	within, inside	intramural, intravenous
mal-	bad, badly	malfunction, maladjusted
mis-	wrongly, badly	misplace, miscalculate
mono-	one, single	monologue, monotone
non-	not, the opposite of	nonsense, nonessential

(continued)

K
E
Y

2

Prefix	Meaning	Examples
post-	after	postpone, postgame
pre-	before	prefix, prepay
re-	again, back	revisit, reattach
semi-	half	semicircle, semiannual
sub-	under, less than	submarine, substandard
super-	above, greater than	superior, superpower
trans-	over, across	transfer, transatlantic
tri-	three	tricycle, triangle
un-	not	unusual, unsatisfactory
uni-	one, single	uniform, unilateral

Suffixes Come at the End

A *suffix* is a syllable or group of letters added to the end of a base word to create a new word. The suffixes *-s* and *-es* turn singular nouns into plural nouns: *coat* + *-s* = *coats*, and *clash* + *-es* = *clashes*. The familiar suffixes *-ed* and *-ing* are added to verbs to change their tense: *create* + *-ed* = *created; wear* + *-ing* = *wearing*.

Suffixes also change words into different parts of speech:

custom (noun) + -ize = customize (verb)

accident (noun) + -al = accidental (adjective)

wise (adjective) + -dom = wisdom (noun)

Suffixes have meanings, too, but learning them is not necessary. Just remember that some suffixes make words into nouns, and other suffixes turn words into verbs, adjectives, or adverbs.

Suffixes That Form Nouns	
Suffix	**Examples**
-age	postage, marriage
-ance	performance, hindrance
-ant	defendant, occupant
-arch	monarch, patriarch
-dom	kingdom, wisdom
-ee	employee, absentee
-eer	mountaineer, charioteer
-er, -or	dancer, actor
-ence	excellence, conference
-hood	childhood, motherhood
-ion	union, inspection, tension
-ism	patriotism, Impressionism
-ment	enjoyment, attachment
-ness	happiness, darkness
-tion	application, demonstration

Suffixes That Form Verbs	
Suffix	**Examples**
-ate	vaccinate, cooperate
-en	brighten, strengthen
-ing	puzzling, keeping
-ize	fantasize, crystallize

Suffixes That Form Adjectives	
-able	capable, reliable
-er, -est	finer, finest; younger, youngest
-ful	hopeful, fanciful
-ic, -ical	comic, magical
-ish	foolish, reddish
-ive	massive, creative
-less	fearless, tireless
-some	handsome, lonesome

Suffixes That Form Adverbs	
-ly	carefully, happily
-ward	inward, outward
-ways	sideways, frontways
-wise	lengthwise, clockwise

KEY 2

Exceptions to the Rule

When you add a prefix to a base word, the spelling of the base word doesn't change. Just add the prefix at the beginning:

dis- + similar = dissimilar   ir- + responsible = irresponsible

But suffixes are tricky. Adding a suffix very often requires a change in spelling. You need to know these spelling rules and, of course, their exceptions.

- Do not change the spelling of a base word if you add the prefix -*ly* or -*ness*.

friend + -ly = friendly   late + -ness = lateness

EXCEPTIONS: In words ending in *y*, the *y* often changes to *i*: *easily, happiness*.

- Drop a silent *e* at the end of a base word when you add a suffix that starts with a vowel.

sincere + -ity = sincerity   move + -able = movable

EXCEPTIONS: There are many exceptions, including *courageous, mileage*, and *noticeable*.

- Keep a silent *e* at the end of a base word when you add a suffix that begins with a consonant.

care + -less = careless   amuse + -ment = amusement

EXCEPTIONS: *argument, truly, nobly*

Double the final consonant before adding a suffix that begins with a vowel. Do this *only* if the base word has one syllable or is accented on the last syllable or if the base word ends in a consonant preceded by a single vowel.

win + -er = winner   hop + -ing = hopping

If you're in doubt about how to spell a word, use a dictionary. See, for example, the mini-dictionary at the back of this book.

Ready, Set, REVIEW

Finding Roots, Prefixes, Suffixes, and More

1. Look for base words, roots, combining forms, prefixes, and suffixes in each of the italicized words below. Use the information in this chapter to make a guess about the meaning of each word. Check your guess in a dictionary, and then write an original sentence for each italicized word.

- Have you read Benjamin Franklin's or Thomas Jefferson's *autobiography*?
- Anne-Marie, an *anthropologist*, is interested in the mound builders, American Indians who built burial mounds and other earthworks.
- Maya's chicken curry recipe calls for many spices and a *judicious* use of hot peppers.
- Ever since he looked at a drop of pond water through a microscope, Ross has been interested in studying *microbiology*.
- Another name for rabies is *hydrophobia* because people with rabies are unable to swallow liquids.
- No matter what anyone says, Howard seems totally *insensitive* to criticism of his paintings.
- Jack says he has a *recurrent* dream about coming to school in his pajamas.
- The chamber of commerce issued its annual *projection* of tourism figures.
- From the three witches, Macbeth gained some *foreknowledge* of what would happen to him.
- Mescal signed up for a *mini-workshop* on peer mediation.

2. Try to think of at least one more word as an example of each root in the chart on page 18.

   You can mix and match the combining forms in the chart on page 19 to form many English words. See how many words you can think of, and compare your list with your classmates' lists.

   Turn to "The Ultimate Word List" at the back of this book. Try to find ten words that start with prefixes. Then, find ten different words that end with suffixes. Compare your lists with your classmates'.

KEY 3

USE CONTEXT CLUES

✓ **General Context**

✓ **Definitions in Context**

✓ **Other Clues to Meaning**

> *How often do you stop reading to look up a new word in a dictionary? If you're like most readers, you almost never stop.*

You have reading detective skills that help you guess the meaning of unfamiliar words. And how do you manage to do that? Probably you've never thought about *how* you do it—you just *do* it. This chapter shows you some useful strategies for figuring out the meaning of new words.

General Context

Words don't travel alone. Every word sits in the middle of its *context*, the words and sentences that surround it. As an experienced reader, you've learned to look for context clues. Sometimes you have to look at the big picture—you may have to read an entire paragraph or more. In the following paragraph, notice the underlined context clues, which help you guess the meaning of *ambiguous*.

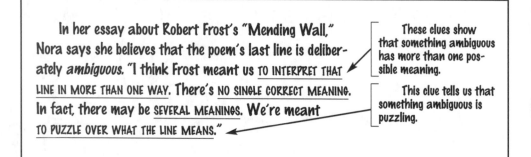

In her essay about Robert Frost's "Mending Wall," Nora says she believes that the poem's last line is deliberately *ambiguous*. "I think Frost meant us TO INTERPRET THAT LINE IN MORE THAN ONE WAY. There's NO SINGLE CORRECT MEANING. In fact, there may be SEVERAL MEANINGS. We're meant TO PUZZLE OVER WHAT THE LINE MEANS."

These clues show that something ambiguous has more than one possible meaning.

This clue tells us that something ambiguous is puzzling.

Definitions in Context

A sentence's structure—its syntax—may provide two kinds of clues:

- An *appositive* is a word or phrase that explains or identifies the noun or pronoun that precedes it. Some appositives are set off by commas. Sometimes appositives begin with the word *or*.

  Every Friday after school, Lara attends a class in *botany*, the study of plants, at the science museum.

The secretary announced the *agenda,* or <u>list of topics to be covered</u>, at the student council meeting.

- Sometimes the definition is a *predicate nominative* (also called a *predicate noun*). A *predicate nominative* is a noun or pronoun that follows a linking verb and identifies or re-names the subject of the sentence. Remember that *is, was, were,* and all other forms of the verb *be* are linking verbs.

    Psychology is <u>the science that deals with the human mind and emotions</u>.

Grammar Clues from the Author to You

Writers often try to help you figure out the meaning of a difficult word. Sometimes they provide a *definition* or *restatement* of an unfamiliar word. The word's meaning is built right in to the sentence, and all you have to do is look for it. For example, the underlined word below actually defines the word *indigenous.*

Can you name some of the trees that are *indigenous,* or <u>native</u>, to your state?

K E Y 3

Other Clues to Meaning

On the next several pages, you can find a number of other kinds of context clues.

Key Words to Clue You In

Key words are the most important words, the ones that help you find precisely what you're looking for. You use key words whenever you do an Internet search. You can tell that a word is a key word if it's repeated often or if it sounds important. Sometimes the structure of the sentence helps you recognize a key word.

About one sixth of the 120 species of <u>SNAKES</u> in America are *venomous.* If a <u>VENOMOUS SNAKE BITES</u> you, go to a <u>DOCTOR OR HOSPITAL IMMEDIATELY.</u>	The key words *snakes, bites,* and *doctor or hospital immediately* show that *venomous* means "poisonous."

Explanations Through Examples

Another way writers try to help you is by giving examples of an unfamiliar word.

> You'll never see a living <u>dinosaur, mastodon,</u> or <u>wooly mammoth</u> because all of those animal species are *extinct.*

Example clues may be introduced with a dash or a colon or with the words *for example, for instance,* or *such as.*

> You can recognize *conifers*—such as <u>pine, fir, cedar,</u> and <u>spruce</u>—by their seed-bearing cones.

Comparisons with Familiar Words

When writers *compare* two things, they show how they are alike. One kind of comparison clue is a *synonym,* a word that has the same or nearly the same meaning as the unfamiliar word. *Enormous, gigantic,* and *huge,* for instance, are synonyms for *colossal.*

Gina built a *colossal* snowman. It was so <u>enormous</u> that she had to stand on a chair to decorate its face.

In another kind of comparison clue, familiar words in a nearby clause or phrase help to explain an unfamiliar word.

My friend Bobbie is a *pessimist.* In every situation, she <u>always thinks that the worst will happen.</u>

Contrasts with Familiar Words

When you *contrast* two or more things, you show how they are different. Writers sometimes provide *antonyms*, words with the opposite meaning, as context clues.

> Dave warned us <u>to hurry</u> and <u>not to</u> *tarry* over dinner, or we'd miss the last bus home.

Explanations Through Relationships

Sometimes you can guess a word's meaning from the general situation in a sentence.

> The little boy <u>couldn't speak any English</u>, but he was able to *pantomime* his request, <u>using gestures and body movements</u>.

Connecting words called *conjunctions* may also serve as context clues. *And, but, or,* and *yet* connect ideas that are equal in importance. They are called *coordinating conjunctions.* Words like *although, if, when,* and *unless* connect a less important idea to a more important one. These are *subordinating conjunctions.*

> Latisha is the most *logical* of my friends. She almost always <u>wins an argument because she gives strong reasons</u> to support her views.

GETTING IT RIGHT

Sample Monologue for Reasoning Out the Meaning of a Word

You're curled up on the couch on a rainy day. You're deep into an exciting part of a mystery novel, and you come across this paragraph:

From a distance, Sean could see that the old house looked *desolate* and abandoned. Shutters hung off their hinges, upstairs windows were broken, the paint peeled, the porch sagged, and the steps were totally gone. Around the house, tall weeds and wild grasses grew hip-high. It was an hour after sunset, and the gloomy darkness gave the house a *sinister* look—as if something evil might be waiting inside. Sean shivered with *foreboding*. "Don't go in, don't go in," his cautious self warned. But Sean ignored his inner voice warning of danger. He climbed onto the sagging porch, reached for the doorknob, and stepped into a pitch-black room that smelled of death and decay.

Here's how you might go about puzzling the meanings as you read:

- Wow! That's three words I'm not sure of: *desolate, sinister,* and *foreboding.*

GETTING IT RIGHT

- Let's see. *Desolate* has something to do with looking deserted and also something to do with looking ruined. *Abandoned* is a synonym, I think, for *desolate*. In the second sentence, the writer gives lots of examples of what's wrong with the house. It's a wreck. Does it ever need fixing up!

- I think *sinister* must mean some kind of mysterious evil. The writer sort of defines *sinister* in the same sentence, right after the dash.

- That leaves *foreboding*. I know that *fore-* is a prefix that means "before" or "in advance." I think that the next two sentences have lots of clues that tell me that *foreboding* must mean "a feeling that something bad is going to happen."

What can you do if an unfamiliar word really stops you, and there are no context clues? Remember the dictionary! You can always check the word's meaning in a dictionary at the back of this book.

Ready, Set,

REVIEW

Guess the Meaning

1. Using context clues, write a definition of each italicized word. Notice the clues that help you guess the meaning of each word. When you finish, check your guesses in a dictionary. How close did you come to the dictionary meanings?

- Ryan is so *amiable* that no one has ever seen him in a bad mood.
- After the hike, I was *ravenous*, so I ate two peanut butter and jelly sandwiches, a lot of raw carrots, and two oranges.
- Homer's *epics*—the *Iliad* and the *Odyssey*—tell of the Trojan War and its aftermath. Critics agree that these long narrative poems are among the greatest works of Western civilization.
- Unlike her sister, Wendy is an *optimist*. Whenever disaster strikes, Wendy cheerily believes that everything will turn out okay.
- The most exciting part of our hike was walking behind the *cascade*, or waterfall, and discovering a huge cave.
- Four-year-old Sara doesn't always tell the truth. I've heard her *prevaricate* in order to keep from getting in trouble.
- Carl is so *gullible* that he believes everything everyone tells him—even telemarketers—and everything he reads in the newspaper or hears on the news.
- Not even a professional *sleuth*, or private detective, can solve the mystery of the missing socks.

KEY 3

- The chairman encourages all of his *subordinates*—his assistants and staff members—to submit their suggestions for improving sales.
- Besides the sun and the moon, how many *celestial* bodies can you identify?

2. Choose ten words from the vocabulary lists at the back of this book. Choose words that interest you or words you've never seen or heard before. Write an original sentence for each word (underline the word), and be sure to include context clues in each finish. When you finish writing your ten sentences, exchange your paper with a partner. Then, use the context clues to guess the meaning of each underlined word in your partner's sentences.

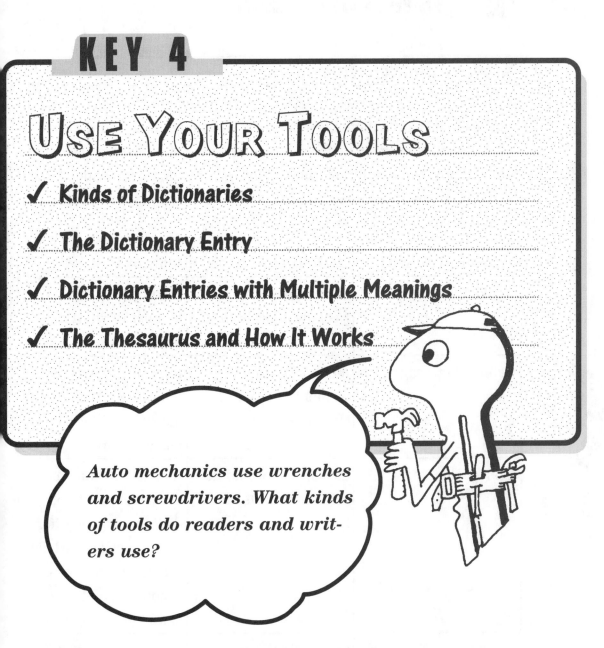

KEY 4

USE YOUR TOOLS

✓ **Kinds of Dictionaries**

✓ **The Dictionary Entry**

✓ **Dictionary Entries with Multiple Meanings**

✓ **The Thesaurus and How It Works**

Auto mechanics use wrenches and screwdrivers. What kinds of tools do readers and writers use?

Carpenters use hammers and saws. Gardeners use spades and rakes and shovels. People who work with words—and you do whenever you read or write—have two handy-dandy tools to help them: a dictionary and a thesaurus.

Kinds of Dictionaries

People talk about looking something up in "*the* dictionary." They really should say "*a* dictionary" because so many different kinds of dictionaries exist. (See, for example, the mini-dictionary at the back of this book. What different kinds of information does it provide about each entry word?) This chart gives an idea of the main types of dictionaries you can come across:

Kind of Dictionary	Definition	What It Does
Pocket dictionary	very small dictionary (usually paperback)	It contains a limited number of words and definitions.
School dictionary	dictionary aimed at elementary school students	It has fewer entries than a college dicnary. Usually, it has many pictures.
College dictionary	dictionary for middle school students and beyond	It contains many more entries than school dictionaries and offers etymologies (word histories), usage notes, synonyms, and antonyms.
Unabridged dictionary	big, fat dictionary (close to three thousand pages) that contains more than 450,000 entry words	It contains more definitions than a college dictionary, fuller etymologies, and citations (quoted sentences or phrases using the entry word).

Kind of Dictionary	Definition	What It Does
Online dictionary	dictionary you can access online	It provides information electronically.
Specialized dictionary	dictionary of words related to a particular subject	Examples include a dictionary of sports terms, a dictionary of slang words, and a foreign-language dictionary.

INSIDE SECRET

College Dictionary

Even though you're not in college, it's a good idea to buy a college dictionary now to use at home. You can use a college dictionary now, in high school, in college, and for the rest of your adult life.

The Dictionary Entry

Dictionaries provide a great deal of information. Look at the following sample entry for the word *sagacity:*

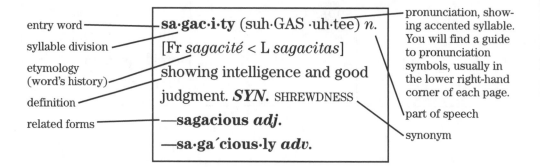

entry word — **sa·gac·i·ty** (suh·GAS ·uh·tee) *n.*

pronunciation, showing accented syllable. You will find a guide to pronunciation symbols, usually in the lower right-hand corner of each page.

syllable division —

etymology (word's history) —

[Fr *sagacité* < L *sagacitas*]

definition — showing intelligence and good judgment. *SYN.* SHREWDNESS

related forms — —**sagacious** *adj.*

—**sa·ga´cious·ly** *adv.*

part of speech

synonym

A dictionary entry may offer many more kinds of information:

- **Usage notes** tell you how—or when—a word is used. Here are some common usage labels:

    arch. = archaic (no longer used)

    Brit. (British) = British

    colloq. = colloquial (highly informal)

    slang = specialized vocabulary (highly informal)

- **Subject labels** indicate that a definition is from *Music, Biology, Radio, Grammar, Mechanics,* or any other specialized field.

- **Citations** show the word in context, usually in a sentence or phrase. A citation is enclosed in brackets or set off from the entry with some other punctuation mark. Sometimes the source of the citation is identified:

    <a knowledge of the *unconscious* activities of the mind
    —Sigmund Freud>

GETTING IT RIGHT

Model Pronunciation Key

Dictionaries tell you how to pronounce words. Look for the pronunciation in parentheses right after the entry word. The pronunciation may contain some special symbols, but don't worry. Dictionaries place a pronunciation key—a guide to the pronunciation marks and symbols—on the bottom of every two-page spread. It may look something like this:

a as in *at;* **ā** as in *play;* **ä** as in *cot;* **e** as in *ten;* **ē** as in *even;* **i** as in *is;* **ī** as in *ice;* **ō** as in *go;* **ô** as in *all;* **oo** as in *look;* **ōo** as in *boot;* **oi** as in *oil;* **ou** as in *out;* **ŋ** as in *ring;* **u** as in *mud;* **ʉ** as in *her;* **ə** as in ago; **sh** as in *shell;* **ch** as in *chew;* **th** as in *thin;* **th** as in *then;* **zh** as in *measure.*

K E Y 4

- **Antonyms** are words that mean the opposite of an entry word.

- Irregular **comparative forms** of modifiers are shown after the entry word:

  good *adj.* **better, best**

- The main forms of **irregular verbs** are shown:

  lie *vi.* **lay** (past) **lain** (past participle) **lying** (present participle)

The keys use *phonetic respellings* to show the pronunciation of a word. Read the pronunciation just as you would read an English word. The accented syllable is the one that's capitalized.

mayor (MAY·er)   **plasma** (PLAHZ·muh)   **radio** (RAY·dee·oh)

Dictionary Entries with Multiple Meanings

Most dictionary entries provide more than one definition, and each definition is numbered. Whenever a word functions as more than one part of speech, the meanings are separated and identified according to part of speech, as in the sample entry below:

> **men·tor** (MEN·tor or MEN·ter) [L < Gr *Mentor*, literally adviser. In Greek mythology, friend and adviser to Odysseus, hero of w *Odyssey*, and teacher of Odysseus's son Telemachus] —*n.* **1.** a wise and trusted adviser **2.** a teacher or coach —*vt., vi.* **mentor** to serve as a mentor; to teach or advise. —**men′tor·ship** *n.*

When you look up an unfamiliar word with multiple meanings, how can you choose the "right" meaning? Try out the different meanings in the context, and choose the meaning that fits best.

> The agency's goal is to recruit 150 new *mentors* for the Boys' and Girls' Club after-school program.

> Mr. Hugh B. Corlett, an English teacher, patiently *mentored* the staff of the *Kirk Spectator*, our school newspaper.

K
E
Y
4

The Thesaurus and How It Works

Thesaurus (thuh·SORE·us) comes from a Greek word that means "treasure," and a thesaurus really is a treasure-house of words. *Thesauri* (that's the plural form) are books of synonyms. They're particularly useful to writers, who search for different ways to express the same idea in order to avoid unnecessary repetition. A thesaurus looks something like a dictionary, but it works in a different way.

Peter Mark Roget (1779–1869), an English doctor, published the first thesaurus in 1852. For almost fifty years he'd been working on a catalog of words grouped according to their meaning. For Roget his thesaurus was a hobby, but when it was published, it sold well.

Here's how a thesaurus works. It's a two-step process. First, you look up a word in the index, which usually takes up more than a quarter of the book. Say you're looking for synonyms for *jar*. Here's what you might find in the index:

> **jar**
>   **n.** container 47.8
>   conflict 102.11
>   shake 234.6
>   surprise 792.8
>   **v.** sound unharmonious 142.7
>   clash 102.09
>   disagree 102.01
>   preserve 52.1
>   shake 146.8
>   surprise 792.9

Suppose you want synonyms for *jar* as a noun, in the sense of the verb *shake*. You turn to the number for the subentry *shake* (146.8), and this is what you find:

> **146.8** shake, quake, quiver, tremble, shiver, shudder; jolt; jerk, twitch; bounce, bump.

Use *synonyms* wisely. Synonyms are words that mean the same or almost the same as another word. For example, *amiable* and *affable* are synonyms that mean "friendly and easygoing." They can be used interchangeably in this sentence:

Jermaine is the most _____ of all my friends.

But synonyms are not exactly alike. To help users see the shades of meaning among synonyms, dictionaries sometimes have *synonymies* at the end of an entry. Here's an example of a synonymy that discusses *amiable* and three of its synonyms:

> *SYN.* —**Amiable** implies friendliness and cheerfulness; **affable** suggests that a person is easy to talk to. Someone who is **genial** is both cheerful and sociable [the *genial* talk-show host]; **cordial** is somewhat more formal, suggesting graciousness and warmth <a *cordial* invitation>.

K
E
Y

4

Ready Set...

REVIEW

Using Your Tools

1. For each italicized word, check a college dictionary to see which definition best fits the context:

   - The Supreme Court is expected to give a *definitive* ruling on the case this fall.
   - Everyone joined in singing the ballad's *refrain*.
   - On the Ellis Island Web site, we found my great-grandfather's name on a ship's *manifest*.
   - Because of the electrical storm, the radio station could not *transmit* for several hours.

2. How much information can you find about each of these words? Compare the coverage in two different dictionaries. Which dictionary do you prefer? Why?

   apex   hurricane   pretzel   pun

3. Use a thesaurus to look up each of the italicized words. For each sentence, list all of the synonyms you can find that you think fit the meaning of the sentence. Compare your lists of synonyms with your classmates' lists.

   - Amra *hurried* down the street, trying to catch her bus.
   - Whenever I tell Sam a joke, he always *laughs*.
   - "Please turn down the volume on that radio," Aunt Lena *said*.
   - A tall young man in a black leather jacket *walked* into the cafeteria.

TACKLE THE TOUGH ONES

✓ **Why You Want to Use Words Correctly**

✓ **Commonly Confused Words**

✓ **Mispronunciations**

✓ **Troublesome Words**

> *As you learn new words, get into the habit of using them when you write and speak. The more words you own, the richer you'll be.*

You can say that you "own" a word only when you can comfortably work it into your writing or speaking. If you regularly practice using some of the words in the mini-dictionary at the back of this book, by the end of the school year, you may own them all.

Why You Want to Use Words Correctly

What's wrong with these sentences?

Trina has a guilty conscious.

Have you seen Evilio's new Web cite?

Ooops—that should be *conscience* in the first sentence and *site* in the second. You want to use words precisely to communicate your thoughts clearly, so people know what you're talking about. When you write, you also want to use—and spell—your words correctly so that readers are impressed with what you know. Mistakes are embarrassing, and teachers take off points for wrong or misspelled words. If you're in doubt, double-check the spelling of a word in a dictionary or "The Ultimate Word List" at the back of this book.

Commonly Confused Words

By now you know when to choose *to*, *too*, or *two*. You also know when to use *bad* (as an adjective) and *badly* (as an adverb). English has lots of word pairs that people mix up—words that sound similar but have different meanings. Learn when and how to use these commonly confused word pairs:

accede, exceed Use *accede* to mean "to agree to something" or "to give in." *Exceed* means "to go beyond a limit" or "to be greater than."

> The city council *acceded* to residents' demands for better street lighting.

> Speeding fines are doubled if you *exceed* the speed limit near a school.

accept, except *Accept* is a verb that means "to agree to" or "to receive willingly." *Except* is a preposition that means "but."

Lauren will *accept* the award for the best original oil painting.

Everyone in the family was at the wedding *except* Jim and Patti.

adapt, adopt Both of these words are verbs. *Adapt* means "to adjust" or "to make changes in order to fit." *Adopt* means "to choose" or "to take for oneself." *Adopt* is most often used to refer to a child's being legally made part of a new family.

It took a few weeks for the puppy to *adapt* to her new home.

Kim has four brothers and sisters; two of them are *adopted*.

affect, effect *Affect* is a verb that means "to have an effect on; to influence." *Effect* can be both a noun and a verb. As a noun, *effect* means "the result of some cause or action." As a verb, *effect* means "to cause" or "to bring about a change."

How will the company's move *affect* your mom's job?

One of the *effects* is that she will have a longer trip into the city.

Studying hard may *effect* an improvement in your grade.

capital, capitol The noun *capital* is the city where the state or national government meets. (*Capital* also refers to an uppercase letter.) The *capitol* is the actual building in which a state legislature or the U.S. Congress meets. Think of the *o* in *capitol* as the dome on the building.

Can you name the *capitals* of Georgia and Tennessee?

We visited the beautiful *capitol* building in Annapolis, Maryland.

compliment, complement The noun *compliment* means "words of praise or admiration." As a verb, *compliment* means "to say words of praise or admiration to someone." *Complement*, on the other hand, has nothing to do with praise. A *complement* is "something that completes a whole."

KEY 5

It's always better to receive a *compliment* than an insult.

What color carpet do you think will *complement* the furniture in this room?

conscious, conscience You can use the adjective *conscious* to describe someone who's alert and awake. *Conscious* also means "aware." *Conscience*, a noun, is that part of your mind that makes you feel guilty when you do something wrong.

Geri was fully *conscious* an hour after her appendix was removed.

Parents try to teach their children to have a *conscience*.

farther, further *Farther* means "more distant." *Further* means "to a greater extent or degree." To keep these two words straight, think of the *far* in *farther*.

> Helena bicycled three miles *farther* than Sam.

> Larry suggested that we discuss the problem *further* at the next meeting.

immigrate, emigrate You *emigrate from*, and you *immigrate to*. You *emigrate* from your home to live permanently in another country. You *immigrate to* a new country to become a permanent resident.

> My great-grandfather *emigrated* from Russia at the age of twelve.

> By 1905, his whole family had *immigrated* to America.

site, cite A *site* is a specific place or location. *Cite* is a verb meaning "to give credit to a source."

> Alan explored the Web *site* of the National Aeronautics and Space Administration.

> In his research paper, he *cited* Web pages of several government agencies. Think of the Works *Cited* list in your research paper.

INSIDE SECRET

Stationary and Stationery

Stationary means "not moving; in a fixed position." *Stationery* is writing paper.

She rides her *stationary* bike for fifteen minutes every morning.

Andie is writing her thank-you notes on light blue *stationery*.

How can you remember which is which? Write a lett**er** on station**er**y.

KEY 5

Mispronunciations

Pronouncing a word correctly can help you spell it right. Here are some common words that are often mispronounced. The underscored letters mark the trouble spots where spelling mistakes most often occur.

accidenta̲l̲l̲y Don't make the mistake of mispronouncing this word "*accidently.*" The suffix -*ly* is added to the adjective form *accidental* (not to the noun *accident*):

accidenta̲l̲ + -ly = accidentally

gover̲nment Pronounce the letter *n*, so you'll remember to spell this word correctly.

gover̲n + -ment = government

labo̲ratory The preferred pronunciation sounds that first *o*. You *labor* in a *laboratory.*

lib̲rary If you don't pronounce the letter *r*, you're likely to spell this word incorrectly. Think of *lib̲ros*, the Spanish word for "books."

mathe̲matics Many people mistakenly forget the *e* when they say and spell this word. Pronounce the *e* so you spell it right.

minia̲ture Don't leave out the *a*. If you pronounce the *a* (the preferred pronunciation), you'll remember to include it when you spell the word.

mischie̲vous Some people make the mistake of adding an extra *i* after the *v*. It's (MIS·chuh·vus), *not* (mis·CHEE·vee·us).

mischief + -ous = mischievous (Note that the final *f* changes to a *v.*)

temperamental Someone who's temperamental is easily upset or excited. To spell this word correctly, make a point of pronouncing the *a* in the middle of the word.

temper<u>a</u>ment + -al = temperamental

vacuum When you push a vacuum cleaner, you're pushing one *c* and two *u*'s. Vacuum is pronounced several different ways, but the preferred pronunciation will help you remember the two *u*'s: (VAK·yoo·um).

Troublesome Words

The English language has many words that seem designed to cause trouble. Among those pesky words are irregular plurals and words that sound alike or look alike but have different meanings.

Homophones: They Sound Alike

Pair and *pear, your* and *you're,* are *homophones*—words that sound alike but are spelled differently. These troublesome word pairs (or triplets, such as *to, too,* and *two*) cause you grief only when you write. When you're talking, no one can tell which word you're using, since the words in a pair sound alike. Some words may not be homophones in some dialects. For example, some people may say these three words in the same way: *bear, bare, beer.* Other people might say those words differently.

Can you define the italicized words—they're homophones—in these sentences? Think about what each word means.

- The *bold* young bowler *bowled* two strikes on her first game.

- From the top *stair,* we could *stare* down at the party.

K
E
Y

5

GETTING IT RIGHT

Irregular Plurals

One *bus* goes by, and then you see two more *buses*—or is it *busses*? You can find irregular plural forms of nouns listed in a dictionary, right after the part-of-speech entry. Here, for example, is the beginning of an entry for *bus:*

bus (BUS) *n.*, *pl.* **buses** or **busses**

Notice that both plural spellings are okay, but the first spelling listed in a dictionary is often the preferred one. So you'd write *buses*. Whenever you're in doubt about a noun's plural form, check a dictionary.

Most nouns form their plural by adding -*s* or -*es* to the singular form. But many nouns don't perform so simply. Here are some types of irregular plurals, what to do when you meet one, and some examples:

Type of Irregular Plural	What to Do	Example
Nouns that change form	Memorize these.	child, **children;** mouse, **mice;** foot, **feet;** ox, **oxen**
Foreign nouns	Check a dictionary.	alumnus, alumnl
Compound nouns	Make the most important word plural.	sons-in-law; sixth-graders; twelve-year-olds
Nouns with the same form for singular and plural	Check a dictionary.	three **fish;** two **deer;** many **moose**
Nouns that have no singular form	Check a dictionary.	**politics, species, news**
Numbers and letters	Add an apostrophe and *s*	three *6*'s; two *m*'s

- Of *course* you need to use *coarse* sandpaper to smooth new wood.

- My *aunt* shrieked when she saw the *ant* sampling her fresh-baked pie.

- Tony *billed* us for the deck we asked him to *build*.

- Many a *fowl* died when the chicken-house roof collapsed after days of *foul* weather.

Homographs: They Look Alike

Just to make things more interesting—and more complicated—English has look-alike words with altogether different meanings. These are called *homographs* (from *homo-*, same + *-graph*, writing). *Homographs* come in pairs. They're spelled exactly alike, but they have different meanings and often have different pronunciations. There are, for example, two kinds of *sewers*. Which one is the (SO·er), and which is the (SOO·er)?

Aunt Edna, who makes all her clothes, is a *sewer* of great skill.
The tennis ball bounced out of the court and rolled into a *sewer*.

Here are some more homographs. How would you pronounce each italicized word?

A mysterious *object* hung from the ceiling.
Do you *object* to this plan?

Julio signed the sales *contract* for the car.
People who *contract* viral pneumonia run a high fever and feel very sick.

K
E
Y

5

Ready, Set, **REVIEW**

Using Words Correctly

1. **You Know These Word Pairs.** Choose three of the commonly confused word pairs below. Define each word in the pair, and use it in a sentence.

beside, besides	lay, lie
between, among	learn, teach
borrow, lend	lend, loan
bring, take	principal, principle
good, well	real, really

2. **More Homographs.** Think of how the words in each of these word pairs can have altogether different meanings. How does their pronunciation change? Use a dictionary for help.

minute, minute	bass, bass
wound, wound	refuse, refuse
invalid, invalid	dove, dove

3. **More Homophones.** What's the difference between the words in these word pairs? Look up their meaning in a dictionary, and write a sentence for each word.

   insight, incite   ascent, assent   faint, feint

BUILD YOUR VOCABULARY

✓ **Memory Tips**

✓ **Making a Personal Word Collection**

✓ **Expand Your Vocabulary**

While You Read

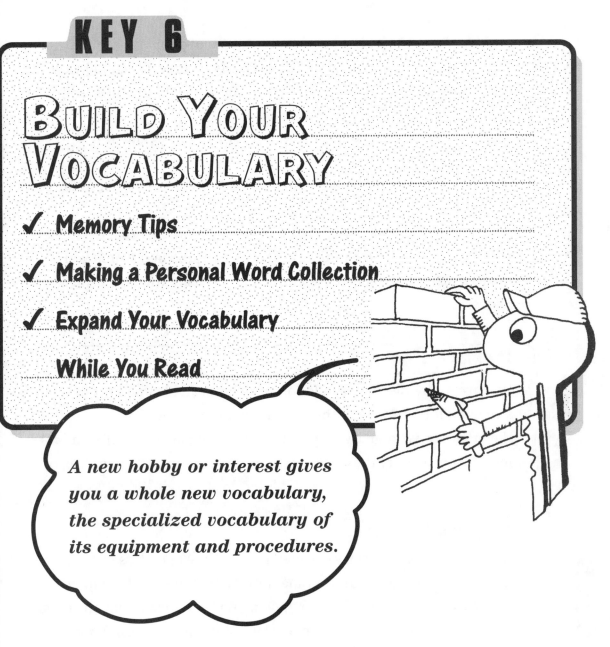

A new hobby or interest gives you a whole new vocabulary, the specialized vocabulary of its equipment and procedures.

As you grow taller and older and stronger, your vocabulary grows along with you. Print materials (books, magazines, and newspapers) and TV and radio continuously bombard you with new words.

Your vocabulary is an important measure of your verbal abilities. In fact, the standardized tests you take usually include a section just for the sake of seeing how strong your vocabulary is. Here's an example:

Directions: Choose the best synonym for the underlined word.
affluence
(a) liquid   **(b) measure**   **(c) wealth**   **(d) importance**

The answer—did you know it?—is (c) wealth. This chapter shows you some strategies for turning challenging words into words you own—words that you can use correctly and easily when you speak and write.

Memory Tips

By now you've discovered a lot of new words and learned good strategies for figuring out their meaning. But how do you "keep" a new vocabulary word? How do you make it part of your working vocabulary? Try these strategies for remembering the meaning of new words.

Make Up a Sentence

Mnemonics (nuh·MON·iks), named for the Greek goddess of memory, is a system for improving your memory. (For example, the sentence **Every Good Boy Does Fine** is a mnemonic for remembering the musical notes on the lines of the treble clef, from bottom to top.) Invent a sentence—either funny or serious—that helps you remember a word's meaning. Here are some examples:

- A garden *slug* moves *slug*gishly—very, very slowly or not at all.

- *Max* was freezing, so he piled on the ***max**imum number of blankets.*

- The S.S. ***Titanic*** was a ***titanic—gigantic*** ship.

- A caterpillar *trans**forms*** itself into a butterfly, an altogether different ***form.***

- The two *l*'s in the middle of *parallel* form parallel lines.

In a confusing word pair, a sentence can help you remember which word is which.

- *Letters* are written on *station**ery**.*

- Look at the *golden d**o**me* on the *capit**o**l* building.

Draw Your Word

Do a sketch that helps you visualize a word's meaning. You don't have to draw well to do this—stick figures are fine. For example, print the word *jovial* in large letters and draw a happy smile in the *o*. Write *dissect*, and sketch a knife down the middle of the word. Write *enigma* on a jigsaw puzzle piece.

Use Flash Cards

Remember flash cards? You can make them from index cards or even small pieces of paper. On one side, write a new word you want to re-

K
E
Y
6

DISCOMBOBULATED

member. On the other side, write a definition and example sentence. Give yourself ten minutes to memorize the definitions in a pile of cards; then test yourself. If you can't remember a word's meaning, turn over the card and look. Make a separate pile of the words you have trouble remembering. Keep reviewing those flash cards until you can easily recall each word's meaning.

Listen to Your Voice

One of the ways you can learn is by listening. Write the word and its definition; then say them aloud to yourself. Make up a new sentence using the word in context, and listen to yourself as you say the sentence. Listening to your own voice reinforces your learning. Saying the words out loud helps, too.

Making a Personal Word Collection

Your teacher may assign new vocabulary words, or you may choose them from your reading. Keep a *vocabulary journal* in a separate notebook or a special section in your notebook. (In your vocabulary journal, you'll record new words that you learn, along with their definitions and an example sentence.) You can even keep your vocabulary journal as a separate document on your computer. In your vocabulary journal, include useful words, words that appeal to you, technical terms, colorful words, strong verbs, and specific nouns. You can even draw a picture of what the word reminds you of or use clip art. Be sure to include any words that tend to be personal trouble spots for you.

Jessie found the word *inflammatory* in a novel she was reading. Here's her vocabulary journal entry:

Vocabulary Journal Entry

Word: inflammatory

Part of speech: adj.

Meaning: causing anger, violence, or great excitement

What I know about the word: It seems to be related to INFLAME, "setting on fire," and FLAME, "fire."

Sample sentence: The audience booed the speaker's INFLAMMATORY remarks.

Another way to learn and remember a new word is to make a *word map*, like the one below. If you work with a partner or small group, talk about a word before you map it:

Word Map

culprit <u>n.</u> someone accused or found guilty of a crime or offense.

What do I know about the word?
- It's not good to be called a culprit.
- It means you're in trouble.

Who could be called a culprit?
- someone who steals
- someone who tricks someone else
- someone who's responsible for another person's injury

What's the opposite of a culprit?
- a hero
- someone who helps or saves others

What are some synonyms for *culprit*?
- villain
- offender

My original sentence: When we found the rug chewed up, we knew that Maggie, our German shepherd puppy, was the *culprit*.

GETTING IT RIGHT

Group Names

Collective nouns refer to whole groups of persons or animals. *Team, jury, crowd,* and *crew* are collective nouns that refer to people. The collective nouns that refer to groups of animals are fun to learn and use. Here are a few examples. Can you find more?

gaggle of geese	colony of ants
pride of lions	swarm of bees
school of fish	troop of kangaroos
pod of whales	clutch of chicks

Expand Your Vocabulary While You Read

In Chapter 3, you practiced using context clues to guess a word's meaning. Chapter 2 showed how analyzing a word's root, prefix, and suffix can help you determine its meaning. Book publishers also try to give you a lot of help. You often find *footnotes* at the bottom of a page and a *glossary* (a specialized mini-dictionary) at the back of a book. Important terms are almost always **boldfaced** (set in dark type) and include a definition in context. If you still aren't sure you know a word's meaning, stop and use a dictionary or ask someone what the word means.

The best way to build your vocabulary is to read and read and read some more. Read all kinds of books for fun. Read the kinds of books that you like best. Read articles in magazines and newspapers. Read what appeals to you. Read online articles and Web sites. Make the time to read, read, and read. Every time you meet an unfamiliar word in context—and context is the important part—you sharpen your ability to learn and remember words and their meaning.

INSIDE SECRET

Word Games for Big Gains

If you like to play word games, you can build your vocabulary by doing crossword puzzles just for fun. You can do them alone, but they're more fun when two or more people work together to guess the clues. You'll find crossword puzzles in daily newspapers and in many magazines.

KEY 6

Ready, Set, REVIEW

Building Your Vocabulary

1. Choose five unfamiliar and challenging words from the mini-dictionary at the back of this book. To learn and remember the words, try using the vocabulary-building suggestions in this chapter:

   - Make a vocabulary journal entry.
   - Make a word map.
   - Do a sketch of the word's meaning.
   - Make up a sentence that includes the word's meaning.
   - Make a flash card of the word and its meanings.

2. Choose a book from the library that you haven't read before. As you read it, write down unfamiliar words whose meaning you can't guess from the context. Stop reading when you've listed five words. Then, look up each word in a dictionary, and write a vocabulary journal entry for each one.

USE THE BEST WORDS

✓ **Substitute Livelier Words**

✓ **Avoid Repetition and Redundancy**

✓ **Avoid Overused Words and Clichés**

So you've added many new words to your vocabulary from your reading. Now what will you do with them?

Make a special effort to use new words when you write and speak. When you do, you sound more interesting, and your ideas sound more grown-up.

Substitute Livelier Words

As you acquire new words, you can start to replace the same old words with livelier ones. Say you're describing something you see—a girl walking down the street. You might write or say:

> A girl is walking down the street.

But that doesn't give the reader or listener a clear picture. If you choose precise words and add some details, you can make the scene come alive:

> A redheaded girl in blue overalls is sauntering down a tree-lined street.

Sauntered is much more precise than *walked*. It describes a particular kind of slow, leisurely walk—the opposite of *hurried*. When writing, use specific, lively words instead of dull, general words.

I WISH I WERE SAUNTERING INSTEAD OF WALKING —I'D BE ENJOYING THIS SO MUCH MORE.

Now you try it. For each of the sentences below, add details and precise, lively words to create a clear, interesting picture for the reader.

The boy and his dog played with a ball.

The sound was very loud.

We went into the water.

When using words in a more refined and precise way, you can also cut down on the number of words you need. One word can be better than many. A single precise word can replace many words, as in the following sentences:

---

raced
I ~~hurried as fast as I could~~ to the door.

pacify
She tried to ~~stop~~ the twins ~~from fighting and calm them down~~.

pianist
Loud applause greeted the ~~person who was going to play the piano~~.

Avoid Repetition and Redundancy

If a teacher says that your work is *wordy*, that's not a compliment. Don't repeat yourself unnecessarily. Say it once, and say it clearly.

WORDY   Whenever Tara feels **nervous,** she starts coughing **nervously** and clearing her throat **in a nervous sort of way.**

CLEAR   Whenever Tara feels **nervous,** she starts coughing and clearing her throat.

When writers use many more words than they need, they're often being *redundant,* or repetitive. Tighten your writing to get rid of the excess. Search for just-right nouns and precise verbs.

K
E
Y

7

GETTING IT RIGHT

Editing

Editing is another word for *revising.* It's a step in the writing process—the one that comes after drafting. As you revise, or edit, your writing, you focus on improving it. Basically, you do three things when you edit:

- delete (take out) unnecessary words, sentences, details, paragraphs

- insert stronger words, sentences, details, paragraphs

- move or replace words, sentences, details, and paragraphs to clarify logic or meaning

REDUNDANT   Julio held his bat as tightly as he could hold it and bobbed it up and down in a nervous sort of way as he watched the pitcher go through all the motions of winding up before he threw the curve ball that he was famous for over home plate.

CLEAR   Julio **gripped** the bat **tightly** and bobbed it up and down **nervously** as he watched the pitcher **wind up** and **pitch his famous curve ball.**

Avoid Overused Words and Clichés

Some words are so overused that they're tired—no, they're exhausted. Avoid these overused words when you write:

Overused Word	Possible Substitutes
very	extremely, quite, extraordinarily, exceedingly (or just leave it out)
nice	agreeable, pleasant, delightful, attractive, considerate
good	excellent, enjoyable, pleasant, fine, splendid
bad	disappointing, unsatisfactory, inadequate, faulty, harmful
terrible	horrible, unacceptable, unpleasant, disagreeable, dreadful
wonderful	marvelous, amazing, excellent, fine, enjoyable
great	excellent, fine, magnificent, splendid, enjoyable

KEY
7

A *cliché* (klee·SHAY) is an expression that's stale from overuse. *Quiet as a mouse, white as snow, cool as a cucumber* are examples. You can probably think of many others. Notice that many clichés compare two unlike things. When you're writing or speaking, try to express your ideas in a fresh, new way—without using overused words or clichés. Sometimes that simply means getting specific:

> **CLICHÉ** Jeff's kitten is *as sweet as sugar.*
>
> **FRESH** Jeff's kitten is so friendly that she curls up on anyone's lap and purrs.

Slang is a highly informal kind of language. There's nothing wrong with using slang when you talk to your friends: "Hey, man, what's happening?" Slang words are fun, and everyone uses them. But slang is inappropriate when you should be using formal standard English. Avoid using slang, for example, when you write an essay or when you speak formally, as in a speech, a debate, or a conversation with an adult you do not know well.

INSIDE SECRET

Watch Your Qualifiers

Very and all of its substitutes are called *qualifiers.* Don't use qualifiers often. Instead, use strong, precise words that don't need qualifying:

She was ~~extremely angry~~.

She was *furious.*

Ready, Set, **REVIEW**

Using the Best Words

1. Write two paragraphs describing what you see from where you are sitting right now. Include many details, and use specific nouns and lively verbs. When you finish drafting your paragraph, edit it carefully. Ask yourself these questions:

   - Have I used precise and lively nouns and verbs?
   - Have I eliminated any unnecessary repetition?
   - Have I expressed my ideas clearly?
   - Have I eliminated wordiness?
   - Have I replaced overused words?
   - Have I expressed my ideas in a fresh way without using clichés?
   - Have I added enough details to give the reader a clear picture?

2. For each of the following italicized clichés, think of a fresh, new way to express the same idea. Write it in a new sentence.

   > I am *so hungry that I could eat a horse.*
   > "Let's *bury the hatchet,*" he said.
   > According to Lauren, the biology test is *as easy as pie.*"
   > "I'm *at the end of my rope,*" she cried. "My computer has crashed!"
   > Raffi's little sister is *as cute as a button.*

3. In the mini-dictionary at the back of this book, are definitions and example sentences for words you should know. Many of those words appear on standardized tests. Take a look, and see how many of those words you already know. How many are completely new to you? Plan a strategy for adding all of those words to your working vocabulary.

K
E
Y

7

Pronunciation Key for the Ultimate Word List

Vowel Sounds		Consonant Sounds	
Symbol	*Key Words*	*Symbol*	*Key Words*
a	at, cap, parrot	b	bed, table, rob
ā	ape, play, sail	d	dog, middle, sad
ä	cot, father, heart	f	for, phone, cough
e	ten, wealth, merry	g	get, wiggle, dog
ē	even, feet, money	h	hat, hope, ahead
i	is, stick, mirror	hw	which, white
ī	ice, high, sky	j	joy, badge, agent
ō	go, open, tone	k	kill, cat, quiet
ô	all, law, horn	l	let, yellow, ball
σο	could, look, pull	m	meet, number, time
yσο	cure, furious	n	net, candle, ton
ōō	boot, crew, tune	p	put, sample, escape
yōō	cute, few, use	r	red, wrong, born
σi	boy, oil, royal	s	sit, castle, office
σu	cow, out, sour	t	top, letter, cat
u	mud, ton, blood, trouble	v	voice, every, love
ʉ	her, sir, word	w	wet, always, quart
ə	ago, agent, collect, focus	y	yes, canyon, onion
'l	cattle, paddle	z	zoo, misery, rise
'n	sudden, sweeten	ch	chew, nature, punch
		sh	shell, machine, bush
		th	thin, nothing, truth
		th	then, other, bathe
		zh	beige, measure, seizure
		ŋ	ring, anger, drink

THE ULTIMATE WORD LIST*

The mini-dictionary on the following pages contains words that are often found on standardized tests. Because the publishers of the SAT (Standard Achievement Test) do not publish a list of the words they use on current tests, the words in this dictionary have been culled from vocabulary lists that appear in several SAT and PSAT test-preparation books. This mini-dictionary also includes a number of words that were judged by the editor of the **Keys to Success** series to be both challenging and appropriate for middle school readers.

Instead of just a word list, each word is given full treatment similar to that in a standard dictionary entry. Notice that each word has a pronunciation guide and a designation for part of speech followed by a definition and an example sentence. For help in pronouncing the entry words, see the pronunciation key on page 72. The centered dots in each boldfaced entry work indicate where a word can be hyphenated.

ab·bre·vi·ate (ə brē′vē āt′) *vt.* to make shorter. *The post office prefers that you abbreviate state names on envelopes.*

ab·di·cate (ab′di kāt′) *vt., vi.* to give up formally (a high office, throne, authority). *Because he is gravely ill, the elderly king will abdicate his throne and allow his son to rule the country.*

ab·er·ra·tion (ab′ər ā′shən) *n.* a departure from what is right, true, or correct. *Grandpa's speeding ticket is the only aberration in his forty-year record of safe driving.*

a·bridge (ə brij′) *vt.* to shorten (a piece of writing) while preserving its substance. *Mrs. Lee abridged the lengthy novel by cutting three chapters so students could finish reading it before the end of the semester.*

ab·stract (ab′strakt′) *n.* a brief statement of the essential content of a book, article, or speech; summary. *I have to write a one-paragraph abstract of my research paper.*

ab·struse (ab strōōs′) *adj.* hard to understand because of extreme complexity or abstractness. *The guest speaker's lecture was too abstruse for anyone to understand.*

a·bun·dant (ə bun′dənt) *adj.* very plentiful; more than sufficient; ample. *The castaways were lucky to find abundant food and fresh water on the island.*

ac·cel·er·ate (ak sel′ər āt′) *vi.* to move at increasing speed. *The driver had to accelerate to pass the slow-moving truck.*

ac·ces·si·ble (ak ses′ə bəl) *adj.* easy to approach or enter. *Federal law now requires buildings to be accessible to people with physical disabilities.*

*Adapted from *Webster's New World College Dictionary*, Fourth Edition.

ac·ces·sory (ak ses´ər ē) *n.* something extra; something added to help in a secondary way. *That blue scarf would be a perfect accessory for your red dress.*

ac·claim (ə klām´) *vt.* to announce with much applause or praise; hail. *The delegates acclaimed the candidate as their choice for the next president.*

ac·cus·tom (ə kus´təm) *vt.* To make familiar by custom, habit, or use. *My friends are accustomed to making themselves at home in my living room.*

a·chieve·ment (ə chēv´mənt) *n.* a thing reached or won, especially by skill, hard work, or courage. *College scholarships are often awarded based on academic achievement and teachers' recommendations.*

ac·knowl·edge (ak näl´ij) *vt.* to show recognition. *My older brother never acknowledges me when we pass in the school hallways.*

ac·qui·esce (ak´wē es´) *vi.* to agree or consent quietly without protest, but without enthusiasm. *She acquiesced to the veterinarian's recommendation that her dog be put to sleep.*

ac·quire (ə kwīr´) *vt.* to get possession of. *The corporation was able to acquire the smaller company for four million dollars.*

a·dept (ə dept´) *adj.* highly skilled; expert. *Elaine and Dave are adept at solving even the most difficult crossword puzzles.*

ad·e·quate (ad´i kwət) *adj.* barely satisfactory; acceptable but not remarkable. *Our campsite is adequate, though it doesn't have a view of the lake.*

ad·journ (ə jʉrn´) *vi.* to close a session or meeting for a time. *Congress adjourned for the summer.*

ad·mi·rable (ad´mə rə bəl) *adj.* inspiring or deserving admiration or praise; excellent; splendid. *Mrs. Rodriguez's effective management and warm approach to students make her an admirable principal.*

a·droit (ə droit´) *adj.* skillful in a physical or mental way; clever; expert. *The detective's adroit questioning exposed the inconsistencies in the suspect's account of what happened.*

ad·van·ta·geous (ad´van tā´jəs) *adj.* favorable; profitable. *Competing on our home field will be advantageous for our team.*

ad·ver·sary (ad´vər ser´ē) *n.* a person who opposes or fights against another. *Someone who knows all your secrets can be a dangerous adversary.*

ad·vo·cate (ad´və kit) *n.* a person who speaks or writes in support of something. *As an advocate of education, our governor is trying to have more money earmarked for schools.*

aer·i·al (er´ē əl) *adj.* of, for, from, or by means of aircraft or flying. *You can see my house from above in the aerial photograph.*

aes·thet·ic (es thet´ik) *adj.* of beauty. *The house that was built atop the waterfall is an architectural and aesthetic triumph.*

af·fa·ble (af´ə bəl) *adj.* pleasant and easy to approach or talk to; friendly. *Everybody enjoys being around my grandmother because she is so affable.*

af·fec·tion·ate (ə fek´shən it) *adj.* full of affection; tender and loving. *A mother's affectionate hugs help a baby feel loved and secure.*

af·fir·ma·tion (af´ər mā´shən) *n.* positive declaration. *I appreciated my* *teacher's comments as an affirmation of my hard work.*

ag·gres·sive (ə gres′iv) *adj.* tending to start fights or quarrels. *Mother bears become aggressive whenever someone or something threatens their cubs.*

a·lac·ri·ty (ə lak′rə tē) *n.* eager willingness or readiness, often manifested by quick, lively action. *The new employee completed the assignment with an alacrity that earned the manager's praise.*

al·ien·ate (āl′yən āt′) *vt.* to make unfriendly; estrange. *I inadvertently alienated her by forgetting her birthday.*

al·lege (ə lej′) *vt.* to assert positively, or declare; affirm; especially, to assert without proof. *Several people alleged that the defendant was guilty of the crime, though none had actually witnessed it.*

al·le·vi·ate (ə lē′vē āt′) *vt.* to make less hard to bear; lighten or relieve (pain, suffering). *New techniques and medications help alleviate patients' pain following surgery.*

a·loof (ə loof′) *adj.* distant; removed. *The woman's aloof manner made it impossible to have a friendly conversation.*

al·tru·is·tic (al′troo is′tik) *adj.* unselfish. *Are we really being altruistic when we help others, or do we do it for our own sake, because it makes us feel good?*

am·big·u·ous (am big′yoo əs) *adj.* not clear; indefinite; uncertain; vague. *The candidate's ambiguous statements left everyone wondering where he stands on important issues.*

am·bi·tious (am bish′əs) *adj.* showing a strong desire to gain a particular objective; specifically, having a great desire to succeed. *Peter is extremely ambitious and will graduate from college in just three years.*

am·biv·a·lence (am biv′ə ləns) *n.* simultaneous conflicting feelings toward a person or thing, such as love and hate. *My brother's ambivalence toward cats comes from his liking but also being allergic to them.*

a·mel·io·rate (ə mēl′yə rāt′) *vt.* to make or become better; improve. *Spending more time on my homework helped to ameliorate the problems I was having in algebra class.*

a·me·na·ble (ə mē′nə bəl) *adj.* able to be controlled or influenced; responsive; submissive. *I was amenable to the idea of leaving early since the lecture was so dull.*

a·mend·ment (ə mend′mənt) *n.* a change for the better; improvement. *An amendment was added to the union contract to improve the workers' conditions.*

am·i·ty (am′i tē) *n.* friendly, peaceful relations, as between nations; friendship. *After the city council settled the neighbors' feud, a spirit of amity returned to the neighborhood.*

a·mor·phous (ə môr′fəs) *adj.* without definite form; shapeless. *As children, we liked to lie outside and imagine animal shapes in the amorphous clouds.*

a·nal·o·gous (ə nal′ə gəs) *adj.* similar or comparable in certain respects. *In many ways, learning to snow board is analogous to learning to surf.*

a·nat·o·my (ə nat′ə mē) *n.* the study of the form and structure of animals or plants. *In biology class, we studied frog anatomy by watching a video.*

an·cil·lary (an′sə ler′ē) *adj.* serving as an aid; auxiliary. *Lawyers may* *consult ancillary sources when the information they have is insufficient.*

an·ec·dote (an´ik dōt´) *n.* a short, entertaining account of some happening, usually personal or biographical. *The writer began her talk with an anecdote about writing her first poem at the age of five.*

an·i·mat·ed (an´i māt´id) *adj.* expressive in a lively way. *My dad's animated account of his adventures in Paris riveted everyone's attention.*

an·nex (an´eks´) *n.* something added on or attached, especially a smaller item to a larger one. *The gymnasium annex will provide the extra room we need for the dance.*

an·tag·o·nism (an tag´ə niz´əm) *n.* hostility. *During the debates, the candidates' antagonism for each other became increasingly obvious.*

an·ti·dote (ant´ə dōt´) *n.* a remedy to work against or neutralize the effects of a poison. *There is no known antidote to the venom of some snakes.*

an·tip·a·thy (an tip´ə thē) *n.* strong or deep-rooted dislike. *Joe can't explain his antipathy for all red foods.*

an·tique (an tēk´) *n.* an item, such as a piece of furniture, made in a former period, generally more than one hundred years ago. *My great-great-grandmother's portrait is now a valuable antique.*

an·tith·e·sis (an tith´ə sis) *n.* the exact opposite. *To her dismay, Ella found her roommate the antithesis of her hopes.*

ap·a·thy (ap´ə thē) *n.* lack of emotion. *He makes no attempt to conceal his apathy toward all things political.*

ap·o·gee (ap´ə jē´) *n.* the point farthest from the earth in the orbit of the moon or of a man-made satellite. *When the moon is at its apogee, its movement slows slightly.*

ap·pease (ə pēz´) *vt.* to pacify or quiet, especially by giving in to the demands of. *The father appeased his screaming two-year-old by buying her candy.*

a·quar·i·um (ə kwer´ē əm) *n.* a tank, usually with glass sides, for keeping live water animals and water plants. *At the Chinese restaurant, Ryan likes to sit next to the saltwater aquarium and watch the fish.*

ar·bi·trar·y (är´bə trer´ē) *adj.* not fixed by rules, but left to one's judgment or choice. *The teacher was unpopular because her decisions so often seemed arbitrary.*

ar·cha·ic (är kā´ik) *adj.* old-fashioned. *Words like* thee *and* thou *are considered archaic because most people no longer use them.*

ar·id (ar´id) *adj.* dry. *The arid climate of the southwestern United States makes it a healthy environment for people who suffer from respiratory ailments.*

ar·ro·gance (ar´ə gəns) *n.* overbearing pride or self-importance. *Alfred is so forceful and confident that some people accuse him of arrogance.*

ar·tic·u·late (är tik´yo͞o lit) *adj.* expressing oneself easily and clearly. *The White House press secretary must be articulate and able to respond easily to reporters' questions.*

ar·ti·fact (ärt´ə fakt´) *n.* an object made by human labor, especially a primitive tool or weapon. *The museum displayed various artifacts from prehistoric times, including tools and weapons.*

as·sid·u·ous (ə sij´o͞o əs) *adj.* done with constant and careful attention. *Newborn babies demand assiduous care because they are so helpless and delicate.*

as·so·ci·ate (ə sōsh´ē it) *n.* a partner, friend, or colleague. *The law firm held a farewell luncheon for its summer associates.*

as·suage (ə swāj´) *vt.* to lessen pain or distress. *My offer to help did nothing to assuage my friend's grief over her dog's death.*

as·ton·ish·ment (ə stän´ish mənt) *n.* the state of being greatly amazed. *You can imagine my astonishment when I heard that my best friend would appear on a TV show.*

as·tron·o·my (ə strän´ə mē) *n.* the science that studies the universe, including the stars, planets, and other heavenly bodies. *While he was taking a course in astronomy, he studied the stars through his telescope.*

as·tute (ə sto͞ot´) *adj.* having or showing a clever or shrewd mind; cunning; crafty. *An astute thinker can quickly analyze and solve a complex problem.*

a·sy·lum (ə sī´ləm) *n.* a place where one is safe and secure; a refuge. *The cathedral offered asylum to the soldiers, who had been marching for days.*

at·mos·phere (at´məs fir´) *n.* the gaseous envelope of air surrounding the earth; the air of a particular place. *The Environmental Protection Agency monitors the gases that factories release into the atmosphere.*

au·dac·i·ty (ô das´ə tē) *n.* bold courage; daring. *The raid demonstrated the guerrilla leader's audacity and intelligence.*

aug·ment (ôg ment´) *vt.* to make greater, as in size, quantity, or strength; enlarge. *We had to augment our research by interviewing more people and consulting additional sources.*

aus·tere (ô stir´) *adj.* very plain; lacking ornament or luxury. *The pioneers' austere lifestyle seems difficult, but it teaches us a lot about living simply.*

au·thor·i·tar·i·an (ə thôr´ə ter´ē ən) *n.* a person who advocates, practices, or enforces strict obedience. *Mrs. Karn, a no-nonsense authoritarian, requires her piano students to practice thirty minutes a day.*

au·to·bi·og·ra·phy (ôt´ō bī ägrafē) *n.* the story of one's own life written or dictated by oneself. *When I write my autobiography, I will focus on my years as a teenager.*

au·ton·o·mous (ô tän´ə-məs) *adj.* having self-government or functioning independently of others' control. *During the American Revolution, some leaders spoke eloquently in favor of an autonomous government, while others remained loyal to England.*

av·a·rice (av´ə ris) *n.* an excessive desire for wealth; greed. *In Charles Dickens's A Christmas Carol, Ebenezer Scrooge is motivated by avarice.*

back·fire (bak fīr´) *vi.* to have an unexpected and unwelcome result; to go awry. *The candidate's strategy of publicizing his opponent's weaknesses backfired by making him look mean-spirited.*

back·track (bak trak´) *vi.* to return by the same path. *To find our way to the car, we will have to backtrack.*

baf·fle (baf´əl) *vt.* to defeat by confusing; to puzzle or confound. *The instructions for assembling the bicycle are complex enough to baffle a rocket scientist.*

balm (bäm) *n.* a substance or method for healing or soothing, especially the mind or temper. *I find that sunshine is a balm for my depression.*

ba·nal (bā´nəl) *adj.* overused; trite; commonplace. *The* Herald *critic gave the movie a poor review, pronouncing both its plot and its characters banal.*

bar·ri·cade (bar´i kād´) *n.* a barrier or obstruction. *The construction workers placed barricades of orange cones around their work space to divert traffic.*

be·drag·gle (bē drag´əl) *adj.* wet, limp, and dirty, as by dragging through mire. *After the storm, the cat's bedraggled coat made her look even more pathetic than before.*

be·fud·dle (bē fud´l) *vt.* to confuse. *I was befuddled until the end of the movie, when all the loose ends were finally explained.*

be·lat·ed (bē lāt´id) *adj.* late or too late; tardy. *Susan never manages to send out cards on time, but she feels that belated birthday greetings are better than none.*

bel·lig·er·ent (bə lij´ər ənt) *adj.* showing a readiness to fight or quarrel. *The hockey coach believed his team's overall belligerent behavior caused frequent fights with opposing players.*

be·muse (bē myo͞oz´) *vt.* to bewilder. *The cabinet's assembly instructions were so bemusing that I finally had to ask someone for help.*

be·nevo·lent (bə nev´ə lənt) *adj.* doing or inclined to do good; kind. *The Key Club, a benevolent organization, planned a food drive for the holidays.*

be·nign (bi nīn´) *adj.* kind; gentle; harmless. *It was a relief when the biopsy showed that the tumor was benign.*

bias (bī´əs) *n.* a mental leaning or inclination; partiality. *Before being chosen to serve on a jury, people are asked to mention any bias that might prevent their assessing the facts objectively.*

bin·ocu·lars (bī näk´yə lərz) *n.* a portable instrument used to view distant objects, consisting of two small telescopes mounted side by side. *Bird-watchers find high-powered binoculars a necessity on their field trips.*

bi·og·ra·pher (bī äg´rə fər) *n.* a writer of someone's life story. *A good biographer carefully researches and interprets facts about a subject's life.*

bi·ol·ogy (bī äl´ə jē) *n.* the science that deals with the study of living organisms; it includes botany, zoology, and microbiology. *Mia is studying biology in preparation for her career as a zookeeper.*

bi·week·ly (bī wēk´lē) *adj., adv.* once every two weeks. *Our school newspaper is so popular that it now comes out biweekly rather than monthly.*

blem·ish (blem´ish) *n.* a mark that mars the appearance, such as a stain, spot, scar. *Just when I wanted to look my best, a blemish appeared on my chin.*

block·ade (blä kād´) *n.* a strategic barrier. *The army set up the barricade to keep the enemy away from the troops.*

blue·print (blo͞o print´) *n.* a photographic reproduction in blue and white, used for architectural or engineering plans; a detailed plan of action. *The team of architects presented the city council with a model and blueprint for the new arts center.*

bol·ster (bōl′stər) *n.* a long, narrow cushion or pillow. *People with back pain are often advised to sleep with a bolster under their knees.*

boom·er·ang (boom′ər aŋ′) *n.* a flat, curved stick that when thrown returns to a point near the thrower. *In Australia, Aborigines use the boomerang for sport and hunting.*

brag·gart (brag′ərt) *n.* an offensively boastful person. *The student's efforts to impress his new friends soon brought him a reputation as a braggart.*

brit·tle (brit′l) *adj.* easily broken. *The archaeologist cautioned her assistants that the ancient fabric was brittle and must be handled carefully.*

ca·jole (kə jōl′) *vt.* to coax using flattery and insincere talk. *I am often able to cajole some people into giving me help by telling them how much I admire them.*

cam·ou·flage (kam′ə fläzh′) *n.* a disguise that uses patterns merging with the background, used especially for troops and military items to conceal them from the enemy. *The colors of army camouflage vary depending on location.*

cam·paign (kam pān′) *n.* a series of organized, planned actions for a particular purpose, such as electing a candidate. *The mayor visited schools, hospitals, and homeless shelters as part of her campaign to get votes.*

can·dor (kan′dər) *n.* the quality of being frank and open. *We were im-*

pressed by the candor with which the celebrity spoke about intimate details of her personal life.

can·tan·ker·ous (kan taŋ′kər əs) *adj.* bad-tempered; quarrelsome. *Children can become cantankerous when they are tired or hungry.*

ca·pa·cious (kə pā′shəs) *adj.* able to contain or hold much; roomy; spacious. *Sam's knapsack is capacious enough to hold his basketball as well as his laptop computer.*

ca·pri·cious (kə prish′əs) *adj.* tending to change abruptly and without apparent reason. *It's difficult to depend on someone who is as capricious as Jane.*

car·bu·ret·or (kär′bə rāt′ər) *n.* a device in which air is mixed with gasoline spray to make an explosive mixture in an internal-combustion engine. *If the carburetor is not adjusted properly, your car will get many fewer miles per gallon of gasoline.*

care·taker (ker′tāk′ər) *n.* a person hired to take care of something, such as a house for an absent owner. *A caretaker looks after my grandparents' home in New Jersey while they are away in Florida for the winter.*

cen·so·ri·ous (sen sôr′ē əs) *adj.* inclined to find fault; harshly critical. *I went to the movie despite the censorious reviews it got from some critics.*

cen·sure (sen′shər) *vt.* to express strong disapproval of. *The judge censured the attorney for using obscene language in the courtroom.*

cer·e·mo·ni·al (ser′ə mō′nē əl) *adj.* of, for, or consisting of ceremony, or ritual; formal. *The queen's role in the country's government is cer-*

emonial, while it is the prime minister who governs.

cer·ti·fy (surt´ə fī´) *vt.* to declare something true, accurate, or certain in a formal statement, often in writing. *Some automobile dealers are willing to certify that their used cars are in good condition.*

chaos (kā´äs´) *n.* extreme confusion or disorder. *Last week's earthquake was so devastating that our city is still in a state of chaos.*

chronic (krän´ik) *adj.* persisting or recurring over a long time. *Dad went to the doctor again because of his chronic cough, which seems to be getting worse.*

cir·cui·tous (sər kyoo´ət əs) *adj.* roundabout; indirect; devious. *We found our way to the party by a circuitous route because of the traffic jam on the highway.*

cir·cu·la·tion (sur´kyoo lā´shən) *n.* free movement from place to place, as of air in ventilating. *Tall bookcases in the conference room interfere with the circulation of cool air.*

civ·ics (siv´iks) *n.* the branch of political science that deals with the duties and rights of citizenship. *Courses in civics prepare high school students to vote responsibly.*

clamor (klam´ər) *n.* a loud outcry; uproar. *When the band finally came onstage, the audience responded with an ear-piercing clamor.*

clan·des·tine (klan des´tin) *adj.* kept secret or hidden, especially for some illicit purpose. *The spy used a code to record details of his clandestine meetings.*

clari·fy (klar´ə fī´) *vt.* to make or become easier to understand. *The scientist was often asked to clarify*

his explanations because of his highly technical vocabulary.

clem·en·cy (klem´ən sē) *n.* leniency or mercy, as toward an offender or enemy. *The governor granted clemency to the death-row prisoner, changing his sentence to life imprisonment.*

co·ag·u·late (kō ag´yoo lāt´) *vt.* to cause (a liquid) to become a soft, semisolid mass. *A bacterium added to milk causes it to coagulate and turn into yogurt.*

co·a·lesce (kō´ə les´) *vi.* to unite or merge into a single body, group, or mass. *When the Revolutionary War began, men from various colonies coalesced and formed an effective army.*

co·gent (kō´jənt) *adj.* to the point, such as during an argument; compelling; convincing. *Can you give me three cogent reasons why I should vote for your candidate?*

co·he·sive (kō hēs´iv) *adj.* sticking together. *The twins' relationship seems more cohesive than the bond between ordinary brothers and sisters.*

col·lab·o·rate (kə lab´ə rāt´) *vi.* to work together, especially in some literary, artistic, or scientific undertaking. *When group work is required, individuals must collaborate to get the job done.*

col·o·nize (käl´ə nīz´) *vt.* to found or establish a colony or colonies in. *In the 1600s, the goal of the early settlers was to colonize the New World.*

com·mis·sion (kə mish´ən) *n.* a fee or a percentage of the proceeds paid to someone, such as a salesperson, either in addition to or instead of wages or salary. *The commission the saleswoman receives for each* pair of shoes she sells makes her eager to clinch a sale.

com·pas·sion (kəm pash´ən) *n.* sorrow for the trouble of others, accompanied by an urge to help; deep sympathy. *His compassion led him to found an organization to help feed and shelter the homeless.*

com·pla·cen·cy (kəm plā´sən sē) *n.* quiet satisfaction or contentment; often self-satisfaction or smugness. *Even though the emergency is over, complacency is inappropriate if the police remain on high alert.*

com·pli·ance (kəm plī´əns) *n.* giving in to a request, wish, or demand. *Inspectors visit restaurants to make sure the food-handling processes are in compliance with the law.*

com·pre·hen·sive (käm´prē hen´siv) *adj.* dealing with all or many of the relevant details. *Some universities require freshmen to write a comprehensive essay describing all aspects of their lives and goals.*

con·cede (kən sēd´) *vt.* to admit as true or valid; to acknowledge. *She was willing to concede the point when she realized his research was stronger than hers.*

con·cise (kən sīs´) *adj.* brief and to the point; short and clear. *Our report must be concise because we have only ten minutes in which to make our presentation.*

con·clu·sive (kən kloo´siv) *adj.* settling a question; final; decisive. *Higher pay was the conclusive factor in deciding whether to move to Georgia or Alabama.*

con·cur (kən kur´) *vi.* to agree (with); to be in accord. *Participants in the contest promised to concur with the judges' final decision.*

con·done (kən dōn´) *vt.* to forgive, pardon, or overlook (an offense). *If you witness a bully's behavior and do nothing about it, then you condone that sort of violence.*

con·fla·gra·tion (kän´flə grā´shən) *n.* a big, destructive fire. *The conflagration destroyed thousands of forested acres in Glacier National Park.*

con·flu·ence (kän´floo əns) *n.* a flowing together, especially of two or more streams. *The confluence of the two rivers forms a navigable waterway.*

con·found (kən found´) *vt.* to make (someone) feel confused; to bewilder; to shame. *I was confounded by the teacher's accusation that I cheated on the test.*

con·sen·sus (kən sen´səs) *n.* agreement; unanimity. *Juries must reach a consensus when deciding their verdict.*

con·straint (kən strānt´) *n.* confinement or restriction. *No matter where she is, Leora voices her opinion strongly and without constraint.*

con·strict (kən strikt´) *vt.* to make smaller or narrower, especially at one place, by binding, squeezing, or shrinking. *If you cut your finger badly, wrap a bandage tightly around it to constrict the blood flow.*

con·tempt (kən tempt´) *n.* the feeling or attitude of one who looks down on somebody or something as being low, mean, or unworthy. *I feel contempt for people who do not stand up for their convictions.*

con·vic·tion (kən vik´shən) *n.* a strong belief; certainty. *A presidential candidate must speak with conviction* *in order to persuade voters that he or she is the best candidate.*

con·vo·luted (kän´və lōฺot´id) *adj.* extremely intricate or complicated. *Josephine's long, convoluted stories are impossible to follow.*

cor·rob·o·rate (kə räb´ə rāt´) *vt.* To confirm, bolster, or support. *The defendant had two witnesses who were willing to corroborate his alibi.*

cre·du·lity (krə doōฺ´lə tē) *n.* a tendency to believe too readily, especially with little or no proof. *Mary's credulity makes her an easy target for pranks.*

cri·te·ri·on (krī tir´ē ən) *n.* a standard, rule, or test by which something can be judged; measure of value. *What criterion did the judges use for awarding blue ribbons?*

cur·few (kʉr´fyoōฺ´) *n.* a time set as a deadline beyond which inhabitants of occupied cities in wartime, or children under a specified age, may not appear on the streets or in public places. *Our city's curfew mandates that anyone under eighteen be off the streets by 9 p.m.*

cy·clone (sī´klōn´) *n.* a windstorm with a violent, whirling movement, such as a tornado or hurricane. *The cyclone destroyed several houses and scattered debris for miles.*

de·ci·pher (dē sī´fər) *vt.* to translate into ordinary, understandable language; to decode. *The baby sitter had to decipher the parents' scribbled notes before she could do what they had instructed.*

dec·o·rous (dek´ə rəs) *adj.* characterized by or showing good behavior or good taste. *We were surprised by the three-year-old's decorous behavior during the wedding ceremony.*

def·er·ence (def´ər əns) *n.* respect accorded to an older person or a superior. *My dad always showed deference to my grandpa's wishes regarding the family business.*

de·flate (dē flāt´) *vt.* to collapse by letting out air or gas. *Gerry drove over a sharp tack which punctured and deflated her front tire.*

deg·ra·da·tion (deg´rə dā´shən) *n.* a lowering in rank, status, or condition. *The manager felt a sense of degradation when he was demoted to assistant manager.*

del·e·te·ri·ous (del´ə tir´ē əs) *adj.* harmful to health or well-being. *Secondhand smoke has been proven deleterious to nonsmokers.*

de·lin·eate (di lin´ē āt´) *vt.* to trace the outline of; sketch out. *Theo has a series of notecards that delineate the main points of his speech.*

de·lu·sion (di loōฺ´zhən) *n.* a false belief or opinion. *George seems to operate under the delusion that he knows everything and is always right.*

dem·a·gogue or **dem·a·gog** (dem´ə gäg´) *n.* a person who tries to stir up the people by appeals to emotion or prejudice in order to win them over quickly and so gain power. *He is a demagogue who plays on the public's fears and insecurities.*

de·nounce (dē nouns´) *vt.* to accuse publicly or inform against. *The editorial denounced the governor after offering evidence that he was directly involved in fraudulent activities.*

de·plore (dē plôr´) *vt.* to be regretful or sorry about. *I deplore the squalid conditions under which migrant workers live and work.*

de·pre·ci·ate (dē prē'shē āt') *vi.* to fall in value or price. *When a car is in an accident, its value depreciates based on the extent of the damage.*

de·ride (di rīd') *vt.* to laugh at in contempt or scorn; to make fun of; to ridicule. *The playground bullies derided the new student's unusual accent until the teacher stopped them.*

des·pot·ic (des pät'ik) *adj.* of or like a tyrant. *Some of the more despotic Roman emperors ruled with ruthlessness and cruelty.*

de·ter·mi·na·tion (dē tʉr'mi nā'shən) *n.* the quality of being resolute; firmness of purpose. *I ran last week's race with the determination of a champion.*

de·ter·rent (dē tʉr'ənt) *n.* a thing or factor that hinders. *United Nations peacekeeping forces act as a deterrent to further aggression.*

det·ri·men·tal (de'trə ment'l) *adj.* harmful. *Cigarette smoking has been shown to be detrimental to health.*

de·vi·ous (dē'vē əs) *adj.* not straightforward or frank; deceiving. *Lara can think of many devious ways to get her younger brother to do her chores.*

de·vise (di vīz') *vt.* to work out or create (something) by thinking; contrive; plan. *Our group tried to devise a workable plan that would combine all of our ideas.*

di·a·lect (dī'ə lekt') *n.* a form or variety of a spoken language, including the standard form, peculiar to a region, community, or social group. *The English dialects spoken in parts of the West Indies can be hard for Americans to understand.*

di·dac·tic (dī dak'tik) *adj.* morally instructive, or intended to be so. *Aesop's fables, such as "The Boy Who Cried Wolf," are didactic stories that can help teach children the difference between right and wrong.*

dif·fuse (di fyoos') *adj.* spread out or dispersed; not concentrated. *It is hard to see in a theater that has diffuse light.*

di·gres·sion (di gresh'ən) *n.* a wandering from the main subject in talking or writing. *The story about her dog was a digression from her original story about working at the animal hospital.*

dil·i·gence (dil'ə jəns) *n.* constant, careful effort. *He deserved to win first place at the science fair since he worked with such diligence on his project.*

dis·as·sem·ble (dis'ə sem'bəl) *vt.* to take apart. *Michael disassembled and rebuilt the engine on his motorcycle.*

dis·cern·ing (di zrn'iŋ) *adj.* having or showing good judgment or understanding. *A discerning reader, Tony organized a book group to read and discuss classic science fiction novels.*

dis·cord·ant (dis kôrd'nt) *adj.* not in harmony; clashing. *The two committees had vastly discordant proposals and were unable to reach an agreement.*

dis·cre·tion (di skresh'ən) *n.* the freedom or authority to make decisions and choices; power to judge or act. *My parents left the decorating decisions in my room to my discretion.*

dis·crimi·nat·ing (di skrim'ə nāt'iŋ) *adj.* able to make or see fine distinctions; discerning. *It's fun to go*

to an art museum with Dave because he's a discriminating critic
and knows a lot about art.

dis·dain (dis dān´) *vt.* to regard or
treat as unworthy or beneath one's
dignity. *Mary's pampered cat dis-
dains all brands of dry cat food.*

dis·in·gen·u·ous (dis´in jen´yo͞o əs)
adj. not straightforward; not candid
or frank; insincere. *She gave a disin-
genuous excuse for not attending
her ex-boyfriend's birthday party.*

dis·par·age (di spar´ij) *vt.* to lower in
esteem; discredit. *It is bad man-
ners to disparage the work of one's
classmates.*

dis·po·si·tion (dis´pə zish´ən) *n.* cus-
tomary frame of mind; nature or
temperament. *Sara has a remarkably cheerful and friendly disposition.*

dis·pro·por·tion (dis´prə pôr´shən) *n.*
imbalance; lack of symmetry; dis-
parity. *There was a disproportion
between the large number of people
who boarded the bus and the seats
available.*

dis·qual·i·fy (dis kwôl´ə fī´) *vt.* to
make or declare ineligible; take a
right or privilege away for breaking
rules. *Drug use will disqualify students from participating in any
team sport.*

dis·sent (di sent´) *vi.* to differ in belief or opinion; disagree (often,
with, from). *Two Supreme Court
judges dissented from the majority
opinion.*

dis·suade (di swād´) *vt.* to turn (a
person) aside by persuasion or advice. *I tried to dissuade my friend
from cheating, but he did it any-
way and got caught by our teacher.*

di·ver·gent (dī vʉr´jənt) *adj.* varying
from one another or from a norm;

deviating; different. *The candidates
attempted to explain their diver-
gent views on important issues.*

di·verse (də vʉrs´) *adj.* different;
composed of dissimilar elements.
*The school has a diverse body of
students from many different
backgrounds.*

doc·trine (däk´trin) *n.* beliefs taught
as the principles or creed, such as
for a religion or political party. *In
the 1840s, the doctrine of Manifest
Destiny was used to justify the ex-
pansion of the United States.*

dog·mat·ic (dôg mat´ik) *adj.* stating
opinion in a positive or arrogant
manner. *I try to listen to the opinions of others and not be dogmatic
no matter how strongly I feel.*

du·bi·ous (do͞o´bē əs) *adj.* causing
doubt; ambiguous. *The suspect's account of what he had been doing
on the night of the murder was
highly dubious.*

du·plic·i·ty (do͞o plis´ə tē) *n.* hypocrit-
ical cunning or deception; double-
dealing. *The duplicity of the
lawyer's demand for strict adher-
ence to the law was revealed when
he was arrested for shoplifting.*

dy·nam·ic (dī nam´ik) *adj.* energetic;
vigorous; forceful. *The dancers'
performance was so dynamic that
the audience felt exhilarated.*

eaves·drop (ēvz´dräp´) *vi.* to listen se-
cretly to the private conversation of
others. *I never meant to eavesdrop,
but I couldn't help overhearing
what they were saying.*

e·bul·lient (i bo͞ol´yənt) *adj.* over-
flowing with enthusiasm and high
spirits; exuberant. *When Kathy is
in a good mood, she is so ebullient
that everyone around her feels
happy.*

ec·cen·tric (ək sen´trik) *adj.* out of the ordinary; unconventional. *Her eccentric style of dress includes feather boas worn with sneakers.*

e·c·lec·tic (ek lek´tik) *adj.* composed of material gathered from various sources or systems. *I have an eclectic collection of rocks that come from all over the world.*

e·clipse (i klips´) *n.* the partial or total obscuring of one celestial body by another, especially of the sun when the moon comes between it and the earth. *We were warned not to look at the sun during the eclipse.*

e·go·tism (ē´gō tiz´əm) *n.* constant, excessive reference to oneself in speaking or writing; self-conceit. *Jeffrey's egotism is so extreme that he believes everything we do is related to him.*

e·gre·gious (ē grē´jəs) *adj.* remarkably bad. *Being an hour late for an interview is an egregious error that may cost you the job.*

e·late (ē lāt´) *vt.* to raise the spirits of; make very proud, happy, or joyful. *Ross's parents were elated by his much-improved report card.*

el·o·quence (el´ə kwəns) *n.* speech or writing that is vivid, forceful, fluent, graceful, and persuasive. *Because she spoke with such eloquence, everyone stayed to listen despite the late hour.*

em·bel·lish (em bel´ish) *vt.* to decorate or improve by adding detail; ornament; adorn. *My little brother embellishes the truth by exaggerating every detail.*

em·i·grate (em´i grāt´) *vi.* to leave one country or region to settle in another. *Kathleen's grandparents emigrated from Ireland to the United States during the 1920s.*

em·u·late (em´yōō lāt´) *vt.* to imitate an admired person or thing. *I try to emulate my older brother Larry, who is honest, reliable, and hardworking.*

en·dorse (en dôrs´) *vt.* to give approval to; support; sanction; to sign as payee on the back of a check or money order. *Each of the candidates at the convention is trying to get the trade union to endorse him.*

en·er·vate (en´ər vāt´) *vt.* to deprive of strength, force, vigor; weaken physically, mentally, or morally. *John's cold enervated him so much that he stayed in bed for two days.*

e·nig·ma (i nig´mə) *n.* a perplexing, usually ambiguous, statement; riddle. *Archaeologists have long pondered the enigma of how ancient Egyptians constructed the pyramids without modern tools.*

e·phem·er·al (e fem´ər əl) *adj.* lasting only one day; short-lived. *Biology students use fruit flies, which have ephemeral life cycles, to study genetics.*

e·piph·a·ny (ē pif´ə nē) *n.* a moment of sudden intuitive understanding or a flash of insight. *Watching the sunset, I had an epiphany about our humble place in the universe.*

e·qua·nim·i·ty (ek´wə nim´ə tē) *n.* the quality of remaining calm and undisturbed; evenness of mind or temper. *She was able to receive the news with equanimity because she had prepared herself for the worst.*

e·quiv·o·cal (ē kwiv´ə kəl) *adj.* uncertain; undecided; doubtful. *The witness's testimony was so full of contradictions that the defendant's fate remained as equivocal as ever.*

er·u·dite (er´yōō dīt´) *adj.* having or showing a wide knowledge gained from reading; learned; scholarly. *Her erudite account of Roman history testifies to her years of study.*

es·o·teric (es´ə ter´ik) *adj.* beyond the understanding or knowledge of most people; abstruse. *Hieroglyphics, the esoteric writing system of ancient Egypt, uses pictures and symbols to represent words, syllables, and sounds.*

eu·phe·mism (yoo´fə miz´əm) *n.* a word or phrase that is less expressive or direct but considered less distasteful or less offensive than another. *Aunt Sadie likes to call a spade a spade and despises the use of euphemisms.*

ex·alt (eg zôlt´) *vt.* to raise on high; elevate; lift up. *The stories of the hero's great feats exalted his reputation.*

ex·e·cute (ek´si kyoot´) *vt.* to follow out or carry out; perform; fulfill. *When the president of the United States gives an order, he expects his wishes to be executed.*

ex·er·tion (eg zʉr´shən) *n.* active use of strength or power. *Anyone unused to intense physical exertion should consult a physician before beginning an exercise regimen.*

ex·haus·tive (eg zôs´tiv) *adj.* leaving nothing out; covering every possible detail; thorough. *Her exhaustive instructions for reaching the picnic site were clear but gave almost too much detail.*

ex·hil·a·rate (eg zil´ə rāt´) *vt.* to make cheerful, merry, or lively; to refresh. *The three things that most exhilarate me are being with friends, dancing, and watching football games.*

ex·pe·di·ent (ek spē´dē ənt) *adj.* useful for effecting a desired result; suited to the circumstances or the occasion; advantageous; convenient. *For Nestor, buying a chocolate birthday cake is more expedient than baking one from scratch.*

ex·pe·dite (eks´pə dīt´) *vt.* to speed up or make easy; hasten; facilitate. *The best way to expedite the delivery of your package is to use overnight mail.*

ex·plic·it (eks plis´it) *adj.* clearly stated and leaving nothing implied. *A person's will should include explicit instructions for the distribution of assets to prevent disputes among surviving family members.*

ex·punge (ek spunj´) *vt.* to erase or remove completely; blot out or strike out; delete; cancel. *Juvenile police records are often expunged when an individual turns eighteen.*

ex·tol or **ex·toll** (eks tōl´) *vt.* to praise highly. *He extolled the pleasures of skiing so much that I am thinking of taking lessons.*

ex·tra·dite (eks´trə dīt´) *vt.* to turn over (a person accused or convicted of a crime) to the jurisdiction of another place where the crime was allegedly committed. *The suspect was arrested in Texas and will be extradited to New York, where the crime occurred.*

ex·u·ber·ance (eg zoo´bər əns) *n.* high spirits; joyous enthusiasm. *He talked about his trip to Africa with such exuberance that it made me eager to travel there.*

fac·ile (fas´il) *adj.* not hard to do or achieve; easy. *We were not satisfied with last week's facile win; we are looking forward to a more challenging game this weekend.*

fal·li·ble (fal´ə bəl) *adj.* capable of making a mistake or being deceived *"We're all fallible," said Mr.*

Sharaka when a student pointed out his spelling mistake.

fa·nat·i·cism (fə nat'ə siz'əm) *n.* excessive and unreasonable zeal. *It's possible to exercise with such fanaticism that you actually injure yourself.*

fas·tid·i·ous (fa stid'ē əs) *adj.* not easy to please; very critical or discriminating. *My boss is so fastidious that I sometimes have to redo my projects many times.*

fa·vor·it·ism (fā'vər ə tiz'əm) *n.* the showing of more kindness and indulgence to some person or persons than to others; the act of being unfairly partial. *One of the players accused the coach of favoritism for always letting Riley play first.*

fea·si·ble (fē'zə bəl) *adj.* capable of being done or carried out; practicable; possible. *The project is feasible, but will require a lot of hard work and planning.*

fe·cund (fē'kənd) *adj.* fruitful or fertile; productive. *Many fruits and vegetables come from California's fecund Sacramento Valley.*

fel·low·ship (fel'ō ship') *n.* companionship; friendly association. *My church group provides the fellowship I need.*

fe·ral (fir'əl) *adj.* untamed; wild. *Residents of the neighborhood have been frightened by a pack of feral dogs.*

fer·vor (fur'vər) *n.* great warmth of emotion; ardor or zeal. *After every hit, walk, or run, the stadium seemed to explode with the fervor of the fans.*

flam·ma·ble (flam'ə bəl) *adj.* easily set on fire. *During a dry season or drought, forests are highly flammable.*

fore·sight (fôr'sīt') *n.* thoughtful preparation for the future. *Experienced campers have the foresight to plan for unexpected weather and other problems.*

for·feit (fôr'fit) *vt.* to lose, give up, or be deprived of, specifically for some fault or crime. *The visiting team had to forfeit the game when their bus had two flat tires.*

fos·ter (fös'tər) *vt.* to help to grow or develop; stimulate. *Charlie credits his uncle as the person who fostered his early interest in science.*

fre·net·ic (frə net'ik) *adj.* frantic; frenzied. *It's exhausting to travel with Robin, who does her sightseeing at a frenetic pace.*

friv·o·lous (friv'ə ləs) *adj.* of little value or importance; trifling; trivial. *I try not to worry about frivolous, insignificant things.*

fru·gal (froo'gəl) *adj.* not wasteful; thrifty; economical. *My dad is frugal and never spends his money frivolously.*

fur·tive (fur'tiv) *adj.* acting in a stealthy manner, as if to avoid being seen; sneaky. *The jewelry store's security cameras recorded the burglar's furtive movements.*

fu·tile (fyoo'tl) *adj.* useless; ineffective. *All efforts to keep the orchestra from bankruptcy proved futile.*

gal·lant (gə lant') *adj.* spirited and brave; courteous and attentive, especially to ladies. *The knight's gallant rescue of the princess from the dragon won him a place in legend.*

gar·ru·lous (gar'ə ləs) *adj.* talking too much, especially about unimportant things. *Aunt Ida is so garrulous that no one else can get in a word.*

gauge (gāj) *vt.* to measure the size, amount, extent, or capacity of.

Weather researchers actually fly into a hurricane to gauge the force of its winds.

gen·er·ate (jen´ər āt´) *vt.* to bring into being; cause to be. *The windmill generates electricity for the farmer's house.*

goad (gōd) *vt.* to prod into action; urge on. *The mule had to be goaded into action.*

gouge (gouj) *vt.* to scoop out; dig or force out. *When it struck the earth, the asteroid gouged a huge crater in the desert.*

gran·di·ose (gran´dē ōs´) *adj.* seeming or trying to seem very important; pompous and showy. *Harriet has grandiose ideas about becoming a writer, but she never sends her manuscripts to publishers.*

grati·fy·ing (grat´i fī´iŋ) *adj.* giving pleasure or satisfaction. *Volunteering at the animal shelter has been hard but gratifying work.*

gra·tu·i·tous (grə to͞o´i təs) *adj.* without cause or justification; uncalled-for. *Phyllis's gratuitous advice annoyed Lynn, who had already made her decision.*

gre·gar·i·ous (grə ger´ē əs) *adj.* fond of the company of others; sociable. *I would have a hard time working alone because I am a gregarious person.*

grov·el (gruv´əl) *vi.* to behave humbly or abjectly, especially before an authority. *I would rather work for less money than have to grovel before a boss who humiliates workers.*

guile (gīl) *n.* slyness and cunning in dealing with others; craftiness. *Some people try to achieve their objectives through guile, but openness and honesty are often more successful.*

gul·li·ble (gul´ə bəl) *adj.* easily cheated or tricked. *I have a friend who is so gullible that he believes everything anyone tells him.*

hack·neyed (hak´nēd´) *adj.* made trite by overuse. *Good writers avoid hackneyed phrases and look for fresh ways of expressing their insights.*

ham·per (ham´pər) *vt.* to keep from moving or acting freely. *Alejandro insists that having a pet will hamper his ability to travel.*

hap·haz·ard (hap´haz´ərd) *adj.* not planned; random. *Her apartment is furnished with a haphazard collection of furniture bought from thrift shops.*

har·bin·ger (här´bin jər) *n.* a person or thing that comes before to announce or give an indication of what follows. *Robins are the harbingers of spring.*

har·mo·ni·ous (här mō´nē əs) *adj.* having parts combined in a proportionate, orderly, or pleasing arrangement. *A choir is considered harmonious when each section can be heard clearly and in tune.*

haughty (hôt´ē) *n.* having or showing great pride in oneself and disdain, contempt, or scorn for others. *The chef was talented, but his haughty manner alienated many customers.*

haz·ard·ous (haz´ər dəs) *adj.* risky; dangerous; perilous. *Smoking is hazardous to your health; it can cause heart and lung failure or cancer.*

heed (hēd) *vt.* to pay close attention to; take careful notice of. *It is important to heed traffic warnings when crossing a busy intersection.*

hei·nous (hā´nəs) *adj.* outrageously evil or wicked; abominable. *The* tyrant's heinous acts of cruelty finally provoked a revolt among the people.

her·e·sy (her´i sē) *n.* any opinion (in philosophy, politics) opposed to official or established views or doctrines In the days of. *Copernicus, it was heresy to say that the earth moved around the sun.*

hi·a·tus (hī āt´əs) *n.* any gap or interruption, as in continuity or time. *After the hiatus of a two-week vacation, the overworked scientist returned to her research with renewed enthusiasm.*

hi·ber·nate (hī´bər nāt´) *vi.* to spend the winter in a dormant state. *Bears hibernate through the cold winter months.*

hin·der (hin´dər) *vt.* to keep back or get in the way of. *His lack of a driver's license will hinder his search for a summer job.*

hin·drance (hin´drəns) *n.* any person or thing that holds back; obstacle; obstruction. *Danny refuses to acknowledge that his bossiness is a hindrance to making and keeping friends.*

ho·mo·ge·ne·ous (hō´mō jē´nē əs) *adj.* composed of similar or identical elements or parts; uniform. *Some people choose to live in a homogeneous community, but I much prefer a neighborhood where different types of people live.*

hos·pi·ta·ble (häs´pit ə bəl) *adj.* the act, practice, or quality of welcoming guests. *When I visited my friend, her parents were so hospitable that I felt completely comfortable.*

hos·tage (häs´tij) *n.* a person taken prisoner by an enemy until certain conditions are met. *The soldier was held as a hostage until the general agreed to release three enemy soldiers.*

hu·mil·i·ty (hyo͞o mil´ə tē) *n.* the state or quality of being humble; absence of pride. *A sense of humility helps us see our own limitations.*

hy·per·bole (hī pʉr´bə lē) *n.* exaggeration for effect. *Saying that someone is "as tough as nails" is a hyperbole.*

hyp·not·ic (hip nät´ik) *adj.* trancelike. *The rhythmic movement of the pendulum had begun to put her into a hypnotic state.*

hypo·crite (hip´ə krit´) *n.* a person who pretends to be what he or she is not. *Elena's father is a real hypocrite-- he spends hours discussing politics but never votes.*

hy·po·thet·i·cal (hī´pō thet´i kəl) *adj.* assumed; supposed. *Imagine a hypothetical situation in which you win a million dollars—what would you do with it?*

hys·ter·i·cal (hi ster´i kəl) *adj.* uncontrollably wild and emotional; possessed by either laughter or fear. *The comedian was so funny that we became hysterical with laughter.*

il·lu·so·ry (i lo͞o´sə rē) *adj.* unreal; producing, based on, or having the nature of a false perception. *She was searching for an illusory Prince Charming like the ones in the fairy tales she had read as a child.*

im·ma·ture (im´ə to͝or´) *adj.* lacking the emotional maturity and sense of responsibility characteristic of an adult. *Carla's boss told her that she was too immature to be promoted.*

im·mi·grate (im´ə grāt´) *vi.* to come to a new country, region, or environment, especially in order to settle there. *My great-grandparents* *immigrated to New York from Italy in 1928.*

im·mu·ta·ble (i myo͞ot´ə bəl) *adj.* never changing or varying; unchangeable. *That night follows day is an immutable law of nature.*

im·pair (im per´) *vt.* to make worse or weaker; damage. *Drinking and driving is illegal because alcohol impairs an individual's perception and judgment.*

im·pede (im pēd´) *vt.* to bar or hinder the progress of; obstruct or delay. *The traffic accident impeded his efforts to get to the meeting early.*

im·pe·ri·ous (im pir´ē əs) *adj.* overbearing, arrogant, or domineering. *The woman's imperious manner angered the others at the meeting.*

im·pinge (im pinj´) *vi.* to make inroads or encroach upon the property or rights of another. *He impinged upon my work space by taking over my desk and answering my phone.*

im·pla·ca·ble (im plā´kə bəl) *adj.* unable to be appeased or pacified. *Peace is difficult to achieve between nations that have experienced decades of implacable hatred.*

im·plau·si·ble (im plô´zə bəl) *adj.* difficult to believe. *Her story of a talking cat was completely implausible.*

im·ple·ment (im´plə mənt) *vt.* to fulfill; accomplish. *The purpose of a fire drill is to test whether people can implement an emergency plan efficiently.*

im·pos·tor (im päs´tər) *n.* a person who deceives or cheats others, especially by pretending to be someone or something that he or she is not. *Some people who pretend to work in phone sales are impostors*

who want the customer's credit card number for their own use.

in·ad·vert·ent (in´ad vurt´nt) *adv.* unintentional. *When I was ready to pay for dinner and leave the restaurant, I realized I had inadvertently left my wallet in my car.*

in·ane (in ān´) *adj.* lacking sense or meaning; foolish; silly. *The joke's punch line was so inane that no one laughed.*

in·au·di·ble (in ôd´ə bəl) *adj.* unable to be heard. *After the microphone quit working, the speaker was inaudible to those in the back of the auditorium.*

in·aus·pi·cious (in´ô spish´əs) *adj.* unfavorable; unlucky. *Losing my wallet was an inauspicious beginning to my vacation.*

in·ci·den·tal (in´sə dent´l) *adj.* happening as a result of or in connection with something more important. *Encounters with celebrities are incidental to my job as a veterinarian.*

in·ci·sive (in sī´siv) *adj.* sharp; keen; penetrating. *Good detectives must have incisive minds to help them solve crimes.*

in·clu·sive (in klo͞o´siv) *adj.* taking everything into account. *As part of the hotel's inclusive room rate, you get breakfast and access to the pool.*

in·com·pa·ra·ble (in käm´pə rə bəl) *adj.* beyond comparison; unequaled. *The opera singer had a voice that was incomparable in its range.*

in·con·gru·ous (in käŋ´gro͞o əs) *adj.* unsuitable or inappropriate; incompatible. *Her cheerful manner was incongruous with the gloomy demeanor of her mate.*

in·con·se·quen·tial (in kän´si kwen´shəl) *adj.* unimportant; trivial. *My bruised elbow seems inconsequential compared with my friend's broken leg.*

in·con·tro·vert·i·ble (in´kän´trə vurt´ə bəl) *adj.* not disputable or debatable; undeniable. *The defendant's story seemed incontrovertible after two witnesses came forward to back up his claim.*

in·cor·ri·gi·ble (in kôr´ə jə bəl) *adj.* that cannot be corrected, improved, or reformed, especially because of previously set bad habits. *Despite having been caught many times, Ana still is an incorrigible liar.*

in·dict (in dīt´) *vt.* to charge with the commission of a crime. *A suspect must be indicted before he or she can be arrested for a crime.*

in·dif·fer·ent (in dif´ər ənt) *adj.* having or showing no partiality, bias, or preference. *I am indifferent to what you prepare, as long as you are the one who makes dinner.*

in·dig·e·nous (in dij´ə nəs) *adj.* existing, growing, or produced naturally in a region or country. *Do you know which Native American tribes are indigenous to your region?*

in·dis·crim·i·nate (in´di skrim´i nit) *adj.* not based on careful selection or discerning tastes; confused or random. *When one makes indiscriminate choices, one can expect disappointing results.*

in·do·lent (in´də lənt) *adj.* disliking or avoiding work; idle; lazy. *The manager fired the indolent employee for failing to stock the shelves on time.*

in·duce (in dōōs´) *vt.* to bring on; bring about; cause; effect. *No one has been able to induce Aunt Kate to share her prize-winning recipe.*

in·ert (in urt´) *adj.* without power to move, act, or resist; very slow to move. *The flu left her inert and miserable.*

in·fal·li·ble (in fal´ə bəl) *adj.* never wrong. *My dad, who has an infallible sense of direction, can find his way no matter where he is.*

in·fa·mous (in´fə məs) *adj.* having a very bad reputation. *That school is infamous for its poor discipline and academic performance.*

in·flam·ma·ble (in flam´ə bəl) *adj.* easily roused, provoked, or excited; easily set on fire. *Jordan struggles to control his inflammable temper.*

in·gen·ious (in jēn´yəs) *adj.* clever, resourceful, original, and inventive. *His card-shuffling machine was so ingenious that it won first prize in the competition.*

in·her·ent (in hir´ənt) *adj.* existing in someone or something as a natural and inseparable quality, characteristic, or right. *His inherent interest in animals made him a good veterinarian.*

in·nate (in´nāt´) *adj.* existing naturally rather than acquired; that seems to have been in one from birth. *The fashion designer seemed to have an innate sense of color.*

in·noc·u·ous (i näk´yōō əs) *adj.* harmless. *I don't understand why she was upset by such an innocuous remark.*

in·no·va·tion (in´ə vā´shən) *n.* something newly introduced; new method, custom, or device. *The new president's innovations upset some people's routines but improved efficiency.*

in·nu·mer·able (i nōō´mer ə bəl) *adj.* too numerous to be counted; very many; countless. *The pioneers sur-*

mounted innumerable difficulties in order to reach Oregon.

in·sip·id (in sip´id) *adj.* without flavor; tasteless. *A variety of spices will make the dish less insipid.*

in·sti·gate (in´stə gāt´) *vt.* to urge on, spur on, or incite to some action, especially to some evil. *I was grounded longer than my brother because I was the one who instigated the fight between us.*

in·teg·ri·ty (in teg´rə tē) *n.* uprightness, honesty, and sincerity. *A person with integrity never cheats.*

in·ter·mi·na·ble (in tʉr´mi nə bəl) *adj.* endless; seeming to last forever. *After an interminable wait, I finally got my test results.*

in·ter·vene (in´tər vēn´) *vi.* to come between as an influence, in order to modify, settle, or hinder some action or argument. *When my sister and I argue, my mother usually intervenes by giving us chores to do in different rooms.*

in·tim·i·date (in tim´ə dāt´) *vt.* to make timid; make afraid. *His arrogance and bossiness did not intimidate me.*

in·trin·sic (in trin´sik) *adj.* belonging to the real nature of a thing. *Food, water, and sleep are intrinsic human needs.*

in·vert (in vʉrt´) *vt.* to turn upside down. *To serve the angel food cake, run a knife around the inside edge of the cake mold and then invert it onto a serving plate.*

in·vet·er·ate (in vet´ər it) *adj.* firmly established over a long period; of long standing. *I dread to think what her lungs look like because she is an inveterate smoker.*

i·ron·ic (ī rän´ik) *adj.* meaning the contrary of what is expressed.

"That's just great!" Marc declared as the vase shattered, but I knew he was being ironic.

ir·res·o·lute (i rez´ə lo͞ot´) *adj.* wavering in decision, purpose, or opinion; indecisive. *Magda is always irresolute about spending so much money and waits until the last minute to buy her concert tickets.*

i·tin·er·ant (ī tin´ər ənt) *adj.* traveling from place to place. *Country people used to buy their few luxuries from itinerant peddlers.*

ju·di·cious (jo͞o dish´əs) *adj.* having, applying, or showing sound judgment; wise and careful. *You will have better luck with your college applications if you are judicious about which colleges to apply to.*

junc·tion (juŋk´shən) *n.* a place or point of joining or crossing, as of highways or railroads. *You'll find the town library at the junction of Main Street and First Avenue.*

jus·ti·fi·a·ble (jus´tə fī´ə bəl) *adj.* that can be defended as correct. *No one thinks that the supervisor's decision to fire him is justifiable.*

kin·dle (kin´dəl) *vt.* to arouse or excite, such as interest or feelings. *Motivational speakers aim to kindle listeners' desires to become more successful and happier.*

kin·ship (kin´ship´) *n.* family relationship. *Though I don't know my cousins well, I still have a feeling of kinship toward them.*

lab·y·rinth (lab´ə rinth´) *n.* a structure containing an intricate network of winding passages that are hard to follow without losing one's way; maze. *In the ancient Greek myth, the hero found his way out of the labyrinth with the help of a string* *that guided him through its twist-ing passages.*

la·ment (lə ment´) *vi.* to feel deep sorrow or express it, as by weeping or wailing; mourn; grieve. *When loved ones die, many people prefer to lament with family members and friends.*

lam·poon (lam pōōn´) *n.* a piece of satirical writing, usually attacking or ridiculing someone. *The novel lampooned the lavish lifestyles of the very rich.*

lan·guish (laŋ´-gwish) *vi.* to lose vigor or vitality; fail in health; become weak; droop. *The plant on her desk languished for lack of water and finally died.*

laud (lôd) *vt.* to praise. *Critics lauded the actors for their ener-getic and sensitive performances.*

leg·a·cy (leg´ə sē) *n.* something handed down from the past, as from an ancestor. *My great-grand-mother's pearl necklace is a legacy I treasure.*

le·thar·gic (li thär´jik) *adj.* abnormally drowsy, dull, or sluggish. *Taking nighttime cold medication can make you feel lethargic the next day.*

lev·i·ty (lev´i tē) *n.* lightness or gaiety of disposition, conduct, or speech; lack of seriousness. *He spoke of the accident with levity, not seeming to care about the car that he hit.*

list·less (list´lis) *adj.* having no inter-est in what is going on about one, as a result of illness, weariness, or dejection. *Diana was so exhausted by her surgery that she remained listless even when her friends came to visit.*

lu·cid (lōō´sid) *adj.* clear to the mind; readily understood. *Mr. Lopez's ex-planation was so lucid that I could*

explain the lesson even to my little brother.

mag·nan·i·mous (mag nan´ə məs) *adj.* rising above pettiness or mean-ness. *It was magnanimous of Toni to offer to shake hands with Julio and forget the whole unpleasant incident.*

ma·li·cious (mə lish´əs) *adj.* spiteful; intentionally mischievous or harm-ful. *Rachel took malicious pleasure in watching the prom queen's fall.*

mas·sa·cre (mas´ə kər) *n.* the indis-criminate, merciless killing of a large number of human beings. *In the movie, the shootout involved a massacre of innocent people caught in the gang's crossfire.*

mav·er·ick (mav´ər ik) *n.* a person who takes an independent stand, as in politics, from that of a party or group. *The newspaper called the politician a maverick because he did not vote along party lines.*

mea·ger (mē´gər) *adj.* of poor quality or small amount. *My sandwich looks meager compared with my friend's lunch of lasagna, salad, vegetables, and dessert.*

me·an·der (mē an´dər) *vi.* to wander aimlessly; to follow a winding path. *The tourist meandered through the Old City, stopping to look in every shop window.*

med·dle·some (med´l səm) *adj.* in-clined to interfere in the affairs of others. *You may think I'm meddle-some for bringing up your prob-lem, but I genuinely want to help.*

med·i·ta·tion (med´ə tā´shən) *n.* deep, continued thought. *I need a period of meditation to sort out my ideas and feelings.*

mer·cu·rial (mər kyŏŏr´ē əl) *adj.* quick, quick-witted, volatile, changeable, and fickle. *My team-mate has a mercurial disposition; he is quick-tempered on the field but mellow afterward.*

me·thod·i·cal (mə thäd´i kəl) *adj.* orderly; systematic. *Every night I follow a methodical routine for getting ready for bed.*

me·tic·u·lous (mə tik´yoo ləs) *adj.* extremely or excessively careful about details. *This essay needs to be perfect, since my teacher is meticulous about spelling, punctuation, and usage.*

mi·crobe (mī´krōb´) *n.* a microscopic organism, especially any of the bacteria that cause disease; germ. *In my lab notebook, I have several drawings of different microbes found in a drop of pond water.*

mit·i·gate (mit´ə gāt´) *vt.* to make or become milder, less severe, less rigorous, or less painful; moderate. *Jenna doesn't feel any better when people tell her that time will mitigate her grief.*

mon·arch (män´ərk´) *n.* the single ruler of a state. *How many countries can you name that still have a monarch rather than another type of leader?*

mon·o·tone (män´ə tōn´) *n.* a succession of syllables of the same pitch. *My English teacher speaks in a monotone that almost puts me to sleep.*

mo·rose (mə rōs´) *adj.* characterized by gloom. *After his puppy ran away, the little boy became morose and refused to play with other children.*

mun·dane (mun´dān´) *adj.* commonplace, everyday, ordinary. *The artist felt he needed a vacation from his mundane routine to renew his creativity.*

na·dir (nā´dər) *n.* the lowest point. *The play's bad press represented the nadir of the author's career.*

neb·u·lous (neb´yə ləs) *adj.* unclear; vague; indefinite. *Jason has no plans—not even nebulous ones—for what he'll do after graduation.*

nem·e·sis (nem´ə sis) *n.* anyone or anything that seems to be the inevitable cause of someone's downfall. *The athlete's nemesis is the third hurdle; she easily clears the first two, but trips on the third in every race.*

noc·tur·nal (näk tʉr´nəl) *adj.* functioning or active during the night. *Most bats are nocturnal and use their hearing more than their vision to find their way in the dark.*

no·mad (nō´mad´) *n.* a wanderer who has no fixed home; a member of a people who move seasonally. *Some early Native Americans were nomads who had to follow their food source—the buffalo—as it migrated across the land.*

non·cha·lant (nän´shə länt´) *adj.* showing cool lack of concern; casually indifferent. *Her nonchalant way of tossing the money down showed that she was used to wealth.*

nos·tal·gi·a (nä stal´jə) *n.* a longing for something far away or long ago or for former happy circumstances. *I still feel nostalgia when I think about my relatives and family home in Georgia.*

no·to·ri·ous (nō tôr´ē əs) *adj.* widely but unfavorably known or talked about. *The deserted neighborhood was notorious for its criminal activity.*

nox·ious (näk´shəs) *adj.* harmful to the health. *The school building was evacuated when several students became sick from noxious fumes.*

nur·ture (nʉr´chər) *vt.* the act or process of raising or promoting the development of; training, educating, or fostering. *The child's natural musical talent was nurtured by her piano teacher.*

ob·du·rate (äb´dοor it) *adj.* not easily moved to pity or sympathy; hard-hearted. *Cinderella's stepmother was obdurate in refusing to let Cinderella go to the ball.*

ob·jec·tion·a·ble (əb jek´shənə bəl) *adj.* disagreeable; offensive. *I find it objectionable when people smoke indoors.*

ob·jec·tive (əb jek´tiv) *n.* something aimed or striven for. *The group's main objective is to complete their assignment on time.*

ob·lit·er·ate (ə blit´ər āt´) *vt.* to blot out or wear away, leaving no traces; erase. *The rainstorm obliterated the chalk drawing we made on the sidewalk.*

ob·scure (əb skyοor´) *adj.* dark; not clear or distinct; faint or undefined. *In the fog, the figures were too obscure for me to see who they were.*

ob·se·qui·ous (əb sē´kwē əs) *adj.* showing too great a willingness to serve or obey; fawning. *She found his obsequious behavior flattering, yet annoying.*

ob·so·lete (äb´sə lēt´) *adj.* no longer in use or practice. *Compact disk players have made audiocassette players practically obsolete.*

ob·sti·nate (äb´stə nət) *adj.* stubborn; unreasonably determined to have one's own way. *The obstinate little boy refused to leave the store until he got what he wanted.*

o·di·ous (ō´dē əs) *adj.* arousing or de-serving hatred or loathing; disgust-ing; offensive. *I thought her behavior last night was odious, and it will take me awhile to forgive her.*

of·fi·cious (ə fish´əs) *adj.* offering un-necessary and unwanted advice or services. *The waiter's officious at-tentions gave us no opportunity for a private conversation.*

om·i·nous (äm´ə nəs) *adj.* of or serv-ing as an omen; especially an evil omen; threatening; sinister. *The sky turned yellow green, and we could see ominous black clouds speeding toward us.*

o·paque (ō pāk´) *adj.* not letting light pass through. *I could not see through the opaque window in the door to find out who was knocking.*

op·er·a·tive (äp´ər ə tiv´) *adj.* of pri-mary importance; key; essential. *In any group project, the operative word that guarantees success is respect.*

op·ti·mism (äp´tə miz´əm) *n.* the tendency to take the most hopeful or cheerful view of matters or to expect the best outcome. *Despite all the troubles she has faced, Mary Jane's optimism keeps her going.*

op·u·lent (äp´yοο lənt) *adj.* showing great wealth. *Although James lives in an opulent home, he prefers to spend time in his friend's small apartment.*

os·ten·ta·tion (äs´tən tā´shən) *n.* showy display, as of wealth or knowledge. *The ostentation of the other woman's appearance made me feel underdressed.*

os·tra·cism (äs´trə siz´əm) *n.* a rejec-tion or exclusion by general con-sent, as from a group or from ac-ceptance by society. *Ostracism by the student council was John's* punishment for failing to attend monthly meetings.

pac·i·fism (pas´ə fiz´əm) *n.* opposition to the use of force under any circumstances. *Some people believe that pacifism is a better way to bring about a change than violence is.*

pan·to·mime (pan´tə mīm´) *n.* any dramatic presentation played without words, using only action and gestures. *Charades is a game in which two teams compete to guess a word or phrase acted out in pantomime.*

pa·ral·y·sis (pə ral´ə sis) *n.* partial or complete loss, or temporary interruption, of a function, especially movement or sensation in some part of the body. *The pinched nerve in my neck caused a temporary paralysis of my right arm.*

pa·ro·dy (par´ə dē) *n.* a literary or musical work imitating the characteristic style of some other work or of a writer or composer in a satirical or humorous way. *The creative writing teacher had her students choose a short story and write a parody of it.*

par·si·mo·ni·ous (pär´sə mō´nē əs) *adj.* miserly; unreasonably frugal. *Though he earns a good salary, Bennett is so parsimonious that he refuses to tip waiters even when he receives good service.*

par·ti·san (pärt´ə zən) *n.* a person who takes the part of or strongly supports one side, party, or person. *She is a devoted partisan of the Republican Party.*

pas·teur·i·za·tion (pas´tər i zā´shən) *n.* a method of destroying disease-producing bacteria (as in milk, beer, or cider) by heating the liquid to a

prescribed temperature for a specified period of time. *Pasteurization destroys bacteria in milk, but some people say the heat destroys the taste as well.*

pa·tron·ize (pā´trən īz´) *vt.* to provide help and support to; to treat in a haughty or snobbish way, as if dealing with an inferior. *She thought she was helping me with her advice, but she patronized me in a way that was humiliating.*

pau·ci·ty (pô´sə tē) *n.* fewness; small number Lots of people come to the shelter to help with. *Thanksgiving dinner, but there is a paucity of volunteers during the rest of the year.*

pen·i·tent (pen´i tənt) *adj.* truly sorry for having done something wrong and willing to atone; contrite; repentant. *Maria wrote a penitent letter, apologizing for the things she'd said in anger.*

pen·i·ten·tia·ry (pen´i ten´shə rē) *n.,* a state or federal prison for persons convicted of serious crimes. *Following the jury's guilty verdict, the judge sentenced the defendant to ten years in the state penitentiary.*

per·pet·u·ate (pər pech´o̅o̅ āt´) *vt.* to cause to continue. *This year's eighth-grade graduates plan to perpetuate the tradition of raising money for a charity.*

pes·si·mism (pes´ə miz´əm) *n.* the tendency to expect misfortune or the worst outcome in any circumstances. *Carl's pessimism means that he is always surprised when anything good happens.*

phan·tom (fan´təm) *n.* something that seems to appear to the sight but has no physical existence. *In the eerie* *dusk, we seemed to see phantoms all around us even though we knew we were alone.*

phar·aoh (far´ō) *n.* the title of the kings of ancient Egypt, often used as a proper name in the Bible. *Tutankhamen was one of the youngest of the pharaohs; he was only nineteen when he was laid to rest in his rich tomb.*

phi·lan·thro·py (fə lan´thrə pē) *n.* a desire to help human beings, especially as shown by gifts to charitable or humanitarian institutions; benevolence. *The millionaire's well-known philanthropy earned him a reputation for being a kind and generous man.*

pi·e·ty (pī´ə tē) *n.* devotion to religious duties and practices; a pious act, statement, or belief. *Jane lives a quiet life of piety and goes to church every day.*

pique (pēk) *n.* resentment at being slighted. *In a fit of pique over being cut from the basketball team, Jose refused to go to any of the games.*

pith·y (pith´ē) *adj.* terse and full of substance or meaning. *The best man finished his speech in a few words with a pithy quote that summed up all our hopes for the couple.*

pla·cate (plā´kāt´) *vt.* to stop from being angry. *The restaurant owner tried to placate the woman who had found a nail in her soup by offering her a free meal.*

placid (plas´id) *adj.* undisturbed; tranquil; calm; quiet. *Mary's placid temperament allows her to remain calm even when there is chaos all around her.*

pla·gi·a·rize (plā´jə rīz´) *vt.* to take (ideas or writings) from (another)

and pass them off as one's own. *Preston got a D on his paper because the teacher saw that he had plagiarized an article he found on the Internet.*

plain·tive (plān´tiv) *adj.* expressing sorrow; mournful; sad. *The plaintive music matched my melancholy mood.*

pli·able (plī´ə bəl) *adj.* easily bent or molded; flexible. *Willow is a good material for making baskets, because when it is wet, it is pliable enough to weave.*

por·tend (pôr tend´) *vt.* to be an omen or warning of. *Those thick, black clouds portend a storm.*

prag·mat·ic (prag mat´ik) *adj.* practical; concerned with actual practice and everyday affairs, not with theory. *The mayor's pragmatic solutions to the city's problems sometimes clash with people's emotional attachments.*

pre·cept (prē´sept´) *n.* a commandment or direction meant as a rule of action or conduct. *A precept I try to live by states that a person should treat people in the same way he or she hopes to be treated.*

pre·cip·i·tous (prē sip´ə təs) *adj.* steep, as in a steep, vertical cliff. *Looking for a challenge, the avid hikers chose a precipitous path up the mountain.*

pre·co·cious (prē kō´shəs) *adj.* developed or matured to a point beyond that which is normal for the age. *The precocious child wasn't interested in baby dolls, building blocks, or any of the other toys usually attractive to children her age.*

pred·a·to·ry (pred´ə tôr´ē) *adj.* of, living by, or characterized by plundering, robbing, or exploiting others. *The cat revealed its instinct for predatory behavior by chasing several birds around the yard.*

pred·e·ces·sor (pred´ə ses´ər) *n.* a person who precedes, or comes before, another. *When Justin started his job, he found that his predecessor had left him a manual of instructions.*

pred·i·lec·tion (pred´ə lek´shən) *n.* liking; partiality or preference (for). *My predilection for rich desserts makes it hard for me to lose weight.*

prel·ude (prel´yōōd) *n.* preliminary part; preface; opening, especially to a musical work. *The soup was an elegant prelude to a delicious meal.*

pre·sume (prē zōōm´) *vt.* to take for granted; accept as true, lacking proof to the contrary. *Supervisors should not presume that their instructions are clear; they should check that their employees understand them.*

prev·a·lent (prev´ə lənt) *adj.* widely existing. *Vast herds of buffalo were prevalent on the Great Plains until they were hunted to near-extinction.*

pris·tine (pris´tēn´) *adj.* still pure; uncorrupted; unspoiled. *No one had been out since the blizzard, and the snow was pristine.*

prod·i·gal (präd´i gəl) *adj.* exceedingly or recklessly wasteful. *The man was prodigal with his inheritance and soon spent all of his money.*

pro·fane (prō fān´) *adj.* showing disrespect or contempt for sacred things; irreverent. *The congregation was shocked by the profane way the old man spoke in church.*

pro·fes·sional (prō fesh´ə nəl) *n.* a person who does something with great skill; someone who earns a living through exercise of a skill. *Christopher, who is the captain of the high school golf team, plays golf like a professional.*

pro·fi·cient (prō fish´ənt) *adj.* skilled. *Secretaries must be proficient in keyboarding since word processing is a large part of their job.*

pro·found (prō found´) *adj.* marked by intellectual depth. *After all this chatter, I long for a profound conversation about things of lasting importance.*

pro·fu·sion (prō fyōō´zhən) *n.* rich or lavish supply; abundance. *The profusion of food at the company picnic satisfied us all.*

prog·e·ny (präj´ə nē) *n.* children, descendants, or offspring collectively. *A family tree is a graphic that shows one couple's progeny.*

pro·gres·sive (prō gres´iv) *adj.* continuing by successive steps. *Her training helped the downhill skier make progressive improvement in her speed.*

pro·lif·ic (prō lif´ik) *adj.* producing young freely; turning out many products of the mind. *His twenty published novels prove how prolific a writer he was during his short life.*

pro·pi·ti·ate (prō pish´ē āt´) *vt.* to win or regain the good will of. *In order to propitiate the company manager, employees arrive at work early and stay late.*

pro·pri·e·ty (prō prī´ə tē) *n.* the quality of being proper, fitting, or suitable. *She questioned the propriety of wearing a short skirt to church.*

pro·sa·ic (prō zā´ik) *adj.* commonplace, dull and ordinary. *Even the* most exciting occupations have their prosaic aspects.

pros·pec·tor (prä´spek´tər) *n.* a person who explores for valuable gold, minerals, or oil. *The gold rush of 1849 attracted many prospectors who hoped to find the valuable ore in California.*

pro·to·type (prōt´ə tīp´) *n.* the first thing or being of its kind. *Engineers create a prototype of a new automobile before they build any that will be sold to the public.*

prov·i·dent (präv´ə dənt) *adj.* providing for future needs or events. *Some provident parents start saving for college when their children are still quite young.*

pro·vin·cial (prō vin´shəl) *adj.* coming from a province; narrow-minded or unsophisticated. *Peter found living in the small town was stifling because people's attitudes were so provincial.*

prox·im·i·ty (präks im´ə tē) *n.* the state or quality of being near. *That overwhelmingly unpleasant smell is a sure sign of the proximity of a skunk.*

pru·dent (prood´'nt) *adj.* capable of exercising sound judgment in practical matters, especially as concerns one's own interests. *I need to be prudent and make good financial decisions if I want to save enough money for college.*

psy·chi·a·try (sī kī´ə trē) *n.* the branch of medicine concerned with the study, treatment, and prevention of disorders of the mind. *To earn a degree in psychiatry, a person must learn how to recognize and treat mental disorders.*

pug·na·cious (pug nā´shəs) *adj.* eager and ready to fight. *I was frightened by the pugnacious tone of her voice and her clenched fists.*

quag·mire (kwag´mīr´) *n.* wet, boggy ground, yielding under the foot. *The hiking trail disappeared in a quagmire that stretched ahead of us for at least a mile.*

quan·dary (kwän´də rē) *n.* a state of uncertainty; perplexing situation or position. *I found myself in a quandary because I wanted to go to the dance, but had already made other plans.*

quar·an·tine (kwôr´ən tēn) *n.* restriction on travel or passage imposed to keep contagious diseases or insect pests from spreading. *During the epidemic, people who had been exposed to the disease were placed in quarantine to prevent others from being infected.*

quer·u·lous (kwer´yoo ləs) *adj.* full of complaint. *Ashley keeps repeating in a querulous tone of voice, "I'm bored! There's nothing to do!"*

quin·tes·sence (kwin tes´əns) *n.* the pure, concentrated essence of anything. *In the movie, the princess was the quintessence of beauty and grace.*

ram·page (ram´pāj) *vi.* to rush violently or wildly about. *Bears can rampage through a campsite, destroying tents, coolers, and backpacks.*

ran·cor (raŋ´kər) *n.* a continuing and bitter hate or ill will. *It is hard to reach a peaceful solution when both parties' hearts are full of rancor from past insults.*

ran·som (ran´səm) *n.* the redeeming or release of a captive or of seized property by paying money or complying with other demands. *The pirates demanded a hefty ransom in* exchange for the safe return of the princess.

rap·port (ra pôr´) *n.* a close or sympathetic relationship; agreement; harmony. *The honest salesman has a good rapport with his loyal customers.*

rat·i·fy (rat´ə fī´) *vt.* to approve or confirm. *Can you explain the process by which states ratify a proposed amendment to the U.S. Constitution?*

rau·cous (rô´kəs) *adj.* loud and rowdy. *After the soccer game ended, the raucous behavior of the fans resulted in some injuries.*

re·cal·ci·trant (ri kal´si trənt) *adj.* refusing to obey authority, custom, or regulation. *The library finally caught up with a recalcitrant patron who had hundreds of overdue books.*

rec·luse (rek´lo͞os) *n.* a person who lives a solitary life, shut away from the world. *I was amazed to see her at the party because she had been living like a recluse since her son died.*

rec·om·mend (rek´ə mend´) *vt.* to suggest favorably as suited for some use, function, or position. *Because I had eaten at this restaurant before, my friend asked me what dish I would recommend.*

rec·ti·fy (rek´tə fī´) *vt.* to put or set right; correct. *Be sure to rectify any errors in your math homework before turning it in to the teacher.*

redo·lent (red″l -ənt) *adj.* smelling (of). *Long after she had left, the room was redolent of the woman's heavy perfume.*

re·dun·dant (ri dun´ -dənt) *adj.* more than enough; excessive. *Some stu-*

dents fill their papers with redundant information to impress their teacher.

regi·men (rej´ə mən) *n.* a regulated system of diet or exercise, for therapy or the maintenance or improvement of health. *To tone their bodies, athletes follow the strict regimen demanded by their coaches.*

rel·egate (rel´ə gāt´) *vt.* to exile or banish (someone) to a specified place. *Because I don't know how to work the new cash register, I've been relegated to the front door as a greeter.*

rel·evant (rel´ə vənt) *adj.* having to do with the matter at hand. *The man's question about when lunch will be served was not relevant to the speaker's lecture about investing in the stock market.*

re·lin·quish (ri liŋ´kwish) *vt.* to give up; abandon. *During the Great Depression, many people had to relinquish their homes and businesses.*

re·morse (ri môrs´) *n.* a deep sense of guilt felt over a wrong that one has done. *I felt immediate remorse when I realized that my rude comment had made her cry.*

re·pel (ri pel´) *vt.* to drive or force back. *Despite the manufacturer's claims, the bug spray doesn't repel mosquitoes effectively.*

re·plete (ri plēt´) *adj.* well filled or plentifully supplied. *The luxurious house is replete with comforts of every kind.*

rep·re·hend (rep´ri hend´) *vt.* to find fault with (something done); censure. *The supervisor reprehended three employees for their habitual lateness.*

re·pris·al (ri prī′zəl) *n.* the act or practice of using force, short of war, against another nation to obtain redress of grievances. *After the war, the victorious nation imposed harsh taxes as a reprisal against the conquered countries.*

re·pu·di·ate (ri pyōō′dē āt′) *vt.* to refuse to have anything to do with; disown or cast off publicly. *I repudiated my former friend after she betrayed my secrets.*

re·scind (ri sind′) *vt.* to revoke, repeal, or cancel (a law or order). *My membership at the gym was rescinded after I forgot to pay my monthly fee.*

res·o·lu·tion (rez′ə lōō′shən) *n.* a determination; deciding. *I have made a resolution to stop teasing my brother.*

res·pite (res′pit) *n.* an interval of temporary relief or rest, as from pain, work, or duty. *By using an ice pack and staying off my feet, I enjoy a respite from the pain in my knee.*

re·ta·li·ate (ri tal′ē āt′) *vi.* to return an injury or wrong. *The peasants stormed the castle to retaliate against the king for his unjust laws and harsh taxes.*

ret·i·cent (ret′ə sənt) *adj.* disinclined to speak readily. *Though she is very willing to discuss her career, she is reticent about her private affairs.*

ret·i·nue (ret″n yōō) *n.* a body of assistants, followers, or servants attending a person of rank or importance. *On the set, the movie star is surrounded by a retinue of makeup artists, hairstylists, and costume designers.*

re·tract (ri trakt′) *vt.* to draw back or in. *The kitten had to retract her claws before she could free herself from the curtains.*

ruf·fi·an (ruf′ē ən) *n.* a brutal, violent, lawless person; a tough or hoodlum. *The villain in the movie was a ruffian who liked to cause trouble in any way he could.*

ruth·less (rōōth′lis) *adj.* pitiless. *The match was brutal; the boxers fought with ruthless ferocity.*

sage (sāj) *n.* a very wise person. *In some cultures, people regard older people as sages and show great respect for their wisdom.*

sal·u·tar·y (sal′yōō ter′ē) *adj.* healthful. *Many recent studies have shown that a diet rich in fruits and vegetables is salutary.*

sanc·tion (saŋk′shən) *vt.* to authorize or permit. *The judge sanctioned the defendant's release on $100,000 bail.*

san·guine (saŋ′gwin) *adj.* cheerful and confident; optimistic; hopeful. *Even though the odds are against us, our coach remains sanguine about our prospects.*

scoun·drel (skoun′drəl) *n.* a mean, immoral, or wicked person. *That scoundrel robbed me!*

scru·pu·lous (skrōō′pyə ləs) *adj.* extremely careful to do the precisely right, proper, or correct thing in every last detail. *The chef is scrupulous about the cleanliness of her kitchen.*

scru·ti·nize (skrōōt″n īz′) *vt.* to look at very carefully; to examine closely. *Before I hand in a paper, I scrutinize it for errors in spelling and usage.*

sec·u·lar (sek′yə lər) *adj.* not sacred or religious; worldly. *Although the concerts take place in a church, the music is secular.*

sed·en·tary (sed"n ter´ē) *adj.* of or marked by much sitting about and little travel. *People with a sedentary lifestyle should try to exercise at least half an hour a day.*

self-con·fi·dence (self´ kän´fə dəns) *n.* confidence in oneself and one's own abilities. *Elaine's self-confidence is evident whenever she engages in a debate because she is never at a loss for words.*

self-re·li·ance (self´ ri lī´əns) *n.* reliance on one's own judgment or abilities. *Good parents teach their children to be self-reliant as they grow up.*

self-re·straint (self´ ri stränt´) *n.* self-control. *Kayla showed remarkable self-restraint when she stopped biting her nails.*

sen·ten·tious (sen ten´shəs) *adj.* expressing much in few words; given to moralizing. *The letter was full of sententious preaching.*

sen·ti·men·tal (sen´tə ment"l) *adj.* having or showing tender, gentle, or delicate feelings. *My grandfather is so sentimental that he saved the ticket stubs from the first movie he and my grandmother saw together.*

ser·vile (sur´vəl) *adj.* humbly yielding or submissive. *Harry considered polishing his brother's shoes to be a servile task.*

sin·gu·lar (siŋ´gyə lər) *adj.* exceptional; unusual. *This dinosaur fossil, a singular example of life in the Jurassic period, is the museum's main attraction.*

skep·tic (skep´tik) *n.* a person who habitually doubts, questions, or suspends judgment upon matters generally accepted. *Ever a skeptic, Victor refused to believe the story as it was told in the newspaper.*

som·no·lent (säm´nə lənt) *adj.* likely to induce sleep; drowsy. *Some medications have a somnolent effect and shouldn't be taken when you are driving.*

so·no·rous (sə nôr´əs) *adj.* having or producing sound, especially sound of full, deep, or rich quality. *Frank was hired as a radio announcer strictly because of his sonorous voice.*

spec·i·fy (spes´ə fī) *vt.* to mention, describe, or define in detail. *I need you to specify when and where you want to meet.*

spe·cious (spē´shəs) *adj.* seeming to be good, sound, correct, or logical without really being so. *He presented a specious argument and lost the case.*

spo·rad·ic (spə rad´ik) *adj.* happening from time to time. *Fire drills at our school are so sporadic that we are unlikely to remember what to do if there is a real fire.*

spu·ri·ous (spyʊʊr´ē əs) *adj.* not true or genuine; false; counterfeit. *Hank Aaron's autograph, which Jay had prized so highly, turned out to be spurious.*

squan·der (skwän´dər) *vt.* to spend or use wastefully or extravagantly. *Environmental activists caution us not to squander water, one of our most precious resources.*

stag·nant (stag´nənt) *adj.* without motion or current; not flowing or moving. *Mosquitoes breed in stagnant water, such as the water that collects in old tires.*

stam·i·na (stam´ə nə) *n.* endurance; resistance to fatigue, illness, or hardship. *It takes a lot of stamina to keep up with two-year-old twins.*

stam·pede (stam pēd´) *n.* a sudden, headlong running away of a group

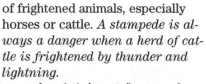

of frightened animals, especially horses or cattle. *A stampede is always a danger when a herd of cattle is frightened by thunder and lightning.*

stig·ma·tize (stig′mə tīz′) *vt.* to characterize or mark as disgraceful. *It doesn't matter how hard she works; her co-workers have stigmatized her as lazy.*

stock·ade (stä kād′) *n.* an enclosure, such as a fort, made with stakes driven into the ground side by side for defense. *The pioneers built a stockade to defend their settlement against enemy raids.*

strand (strand) *n.* any one of the threads, fibers, or wires that are twisted together to form a length of string, rope, or cable. *A rope is produced by twisting together three or more strands of natural or synthetic fibers.*

stri·dent (strīd″nt) *adj.* harsh-sounding; shrill; grating. *From a block away, I could recognize Aunt Martha's strident voice as she scolded my cousins.*

strife (strīf) *n.* the act or state of fighting or quarreling, especially bitterly. *After years of bitter strife, a peace agreement was finally reached.*

sty·mie (stī′mē) *vt.* to hinder or obstruct. *When a crossword puzzle has you stymied, do you think it's fair to use a dictionary?*

suave (swäv) *adj.* graceful and polite. *Because the man exhibited confidence and a suave manner, his speech was well received.*

sub·mis·sive (sub mis′iv) *adj.* having or showing a tendency to submit without resistance; docile; yielding. *Well-trained dogs are submissive to their masters and obey their commands.*

sub·or·di·nate (sə bôrd″n it) *adj.* inferior to or placed below another in rank, power, or importance. *Because I had no experience aboard a sailboat, I was clearly subordinate to those who knew what they were doing.*

sub·tle·ty (sut″l tē) *n.* delicacy; the ability or tendency to make fine distinctions. *The subtlety of her argument convinced me to take her course.*

suc·cinct (sək siŋkt′) *adj.* clearly and briefly stated. *We tried to make the club rules succinct, so that everybody would understand and remember them.*

su·per·ci·li·ous (soo′pər sil′ē əs) *adj.* proud, haughty. *She glanced at me in a supercilious manner that made me feel both embarrassed and angry.*

su·per·fi·cial (soo′pər fish′əl) *adj.* concerned with and understanding only the easily apparent and obvious. *I think my friend is superficial because she says that looks are more important than personality.*

su·per·flu·ous (sə pur′floo əs) *adj.* more than is needed, useful, or wanted. *The directions taped on the microwave door make the instruction manual superfluous.*

sur·feit (sur′fit) *n.* too great an amount or supply. *I miscalculated and wound up with a surfeit of fabric, enough to make two extra blankets.*

sur·rep·ti·tious (sur′əp tish′əs) *adj.* secret, stealthy. *The teacher was angry when she discovered the surreptitious notes the students were passing.*

sus·cep·ti·ble (sə sep′tə bəl) *adj.* easily influenced by or affected with. *If you get a yearly flu shot, you will be less susceptible to illness during the flu season.*

swin·dle (swin′dəl) *vt.* to get money or property from (another) under false pretenses. *The man felt he had been swindled in the card game and demanded that a different player deal the cards.*

sym·me·try (sim′ə trē) *n.* similarity of form or arrangement on either side. *She placed identical lamps on each of the two end tables so the living room would have a pleasing symmetry.*

syn·the·sis (sin′thə sis) *n.* the putting together of parts or elements so as to form a whole. *Because three students worked on the project, the result was a synthesis of ideas.*

syn·thetic (sin thet′ik) *adj.* not real or genuine; artificial. *She is so committed to animal rights that she will wear only synthetic leather shoes.*

ta·cit (tas′it) *adj.* not expressed or declared openly, but implied or understood. *By keeping silent, the audience gave their tacit approval to the committee's decision.*

tac·i·turn (tas′ə tʉrn′) *adj.* almost always silent; not liking to talk. *Farmer Hoggett is so taciturn that his greatest expression of enthusiasm is to say, "That'll do."*

tac·tile (tak′təl) *adj.* related to the sense of touch; perceptible by touch. *Tactile pleasures, such as the feeling of fur and silk, are important to me.*

tan·ta·mount (tant′ə mount′) *adj.* equal or equivalent (to). *Although she did not accuse him directly, her satirical column was tanta-*

mount to an accusation that the mayor had lied.

te·na·cious (tə nā′shəs) *adj.* persistent; stubborn. *Though easygoing in most other ways, Noreen is tenacious in her opinions regarding education and taxes.*

ten·ta·tive (ten′tə tiv) *adj.* not definite or final. *Our plans to vacation in Hawaii next summer will be tentative until we know our schedules.*

ten·u·ous (ten′yoo əs) *adj.* not substantial; slight; flimsy. *The tenuous evidence against the suspect resulted in the police having to release him.*

ter·rain (tə rān′) *n.* tract of ground; the natural or topographical features of a tract of ground. *To strengthen their leg muscles and improve their endurance, cross-country athletes run on rocky terrain.*

ter·ri·to·ri·al (ter′ə tôr′ē əl) *adj.* of, belonging to, or claiming and defending a specific region or district. *Dogs are usually territorial and will growl or bark at strangers or even strange dogs.*

thwart (thwôrt) *vt.* to hinder, obstruct, frustrate, or defeat (a person or plans). *My broken finger thwarted my plans to compete in the tennis tournament on Saturday.*

ti·rade (tī′rād′) *n.* a long, vehement speech, especially one of denunciation. *When she got to the podium, instead of giving the usual complimentary speech, the prizewinner unleashed a tirade about the unfairness of the system.*

tox·ic (täks′ik) *adj.* acting as a poison; poisonous. *Many household*

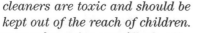

cleaners are toxic and should be kept out of the reach of children.

tran·scend·ent (tran sen´dənt) *adj.* surpassing; excelling; extraord-inary. *People often turn to religion in search of a transcendent experience.*

trans·for·ma·tion (trans´fər mā´shən) *n.* the process of changing. *Butterflies and frogs have life cycles that involve extraordinary transformations.*

trans·fuse (trans fyo͞oz´) *vt.* to transfer or transmit by causing to flow. *The crowd of spectators was soon transfused with the cheerleaders' energy and began joining in the cheers.*

trans·gres·sion (trans gresh´ən) *n.* breach of a law or duty; sin. *His transgression earned the shoplifter a hefty fine and a night in jail.*

tran·si·ent (tran´shənt) *adj.* staying only for a short time. *Most of the boardinghouse guests are transient people with no permanent ties to the community.*

tran·si·to·ry (tran´sə tôr´ē) *adj.* temporary, fleeting. *An adrenaline rush causes a transitory feeling of excitement.*

treach·er·ous (trech´ər əs) *adj.* giving a false appearance of safety or reliability. *While the ocean looks calm, its treacherous riptides are extremely dangerous.*

trea·son (trē´zən) *n.* betrayal of one's country. *Benedict Arnold, an American general, committed treason by trying to surrender West Point to the British during the Revolutionary War.*

trep·i·da·tion (trep´ə dā´shən) *n.* fearful uncertainty or anxiety. *My shaking hands betrayed my trepidation as I approached the snake.*

tres·pass (tres´pəs) *vi.* to go on another's land or property without permission. *When the neighbor caught us in his orchard, he threatened to sue if we trespassed again.*

trite (trīt) *adj.* lacking freshness, originality, or novelty. *In the poem I am writing, I have tried to avoid trite figures of speech.*

u·biq·ui·tous (yo͞o bik´wə təs) *adj.* present everywhere at the same time. *The tall man in the blue suit seems to be ubiquitous; I saw him everywhere I went today.*

un·a·bridged (un´ə brijd´) *adj.* not shortened; complete. *Whenever I listen to a book on audiotape, I make sure it is the unabridged version because I don't want to miss anything.*

un·wield·y (un wēl´dē) *adj.* hard to manage, handle, or deal with, as because of large size or heaviness, or awkward form. *She tried to mail a tuba to her sister but found the package unwieldy.*

u·surp (yo͞o zʉrp´) *vt.* to take or assume (power, a position, property, or rights) and hold in possession by force or without right. *The military usurped control of the government from the elected president.*

vac·il·late (vas´ə lāt´) *vi.* to sway to and fro; waver. *I vacillated for a whole day, trying to decide whether I would research dolphins or orcas.*

vac·u·ous (vak´yo͞o əs) *adj.* having or showing lack of intelligence, interest, or thought. *His vacuous comments show that he has given the matter no thought.*

ven·er·ate (ven´ər āt´) *vt.* to regard with deep respect and admiration. *I* *venerate my sister for being able to manage a successful career as a lawyer while also raising four children.*

ver·bose (vər bōs´) *adj.* wordy; long-winded. *The tour guide's verbose explanation of how the dam was built used up almost all the time we had.*

ves·tige (ves´tij) *n.* a trace, mark, or sign of something that once existed but has disappeared. *The Mayan ruins are vestiges of a civilization that once was great and powerful.*

vice versa (vī´sə vʉr´sə) *adv.* With the order or relation reversed; conversely. *I'll help you when you need it, and vice versa.*

vig·i·lance (vij´ə ləns) *n.* watchfulness; state of being alert to danger. *The security guard's vigilance prevented the robbers from entering the bank.*

vin·di·cate (vin´də kāt´) *vt.* to clear from criticism, blame, guilt, or suspicion. *New evidence in the trial vindicated the defendant; the case was dismissed and he was free to go.*

vin·dic·tive (vin dik´tiv) *adj.* revengeful in spirit; inclined to seek vengeance. *Watch out for Adam—he is vindictive when he loses a game.*

vir·u·lent (vir´yo͞o lənt) *adj.* extremely poisonous or injurious; deadly. *Black widow spider bites are virulent and cause an immediate, painful reaction.*

vol·a·tile (väl´ə təl) *adj.* likely to shift quickly and unpredictably; unstable; explosive. *When I make a mistake, I have to be careful of my boss's volatile temper.*

vol·un·tary (väl´ən ter´ē) *adj.* brought about by one's own free choice. *Because I feel sorry for homeless animals, I make a voluntary contribution to the local shelter often.*

vo·ra·cious (vô rā´shəs) *adj.* very greedy or eager in some desire or pursuit. *It is hard to satisfy her voracious appetite with just one sandwich.*

vul·ner·a·ble (vul´nər ə bəl) *adj.* that can be wounded or injured; open to criticism or attack. *Houses that are built on the ocean shore are extremely vulnerable during a hurricane.*

whim·si·cal (hwim´zi kəl) *adj.* arising from caprice; oddly out of the ordinary; fanciful. *My boss's decisions are often whimsical, instead of based on planning and strategy.*

wran·gle (raŋ´gəl) *vi.* to argue; dispute. *I've used every defensive argument I have and do not want to wrangle with her anymore.*

writhe (rīth) *vi.* to make twisting or turning movements; squirm. *Live worms on a fishing hook writhe and catch the attention of fish.*

yield (yēld) *vt.* to give; concede; grant. *The accident was my fault because I failed to yield the right of way before I turned.*

zea·lot (zel´ət) *n.* a person who has an extreme or excessive devotion to a cause; fanatic. *Lorene is such a zealot about protecting whales that she talks about nothing else.*

ze·nith (zē´nith) *n.* the highest point; peak. *He reached the zenith of his acting career before he was twelve and has been struggling to get back there ever since.*

INDEX